The Divine Openings™ *Playbook*

A Companion Guide
AND Journal
FOR
*Things Are Going Great In My Absence:
How To Let Go And Let The Divine Do The Heavy Lifting*
BY Lola Jones

Melinda Gates

Copyright © 2016, Melinda Gates

All rights reserved. Except for brief quotations in book reviews and articles, and as otherwise permitted by applicable law, no part of this book may be reproduced, used, stored, transmitted or displayed in any form, or by any means (electronic, mechanical, or otherwise) now known or hereafter devised—including photocopy, recording, or any information storage and retrieval system—without prior written permission from: Melinda Gates.
Contact melinda@lolajones.com.

www.DivineOpenings.com
www.AwakeningToYes.com

This book is not intended to replace your own inner guidance,
nor to provide or replace medical advice.

Published by Melinda Gates
Printed in the United States of America

ISBN: 978-0-692-79586-6

Acknowledgments and Appreciation

I offer my everlasting appreciation to the divine Lola Jones for finding her bliss and sharing its address with the rest of us—and for creating such a generous trail of breadcrumbs to keep us pointed in the right direction; to the radiant Donna Wetterstrand, whose boundless love and guidance have illuminated and smoothed the path for me and so many others; to gifted poet and writer Jill Cooper, who graciously helped bring this *Playbook* to life by encouraging and inspiring me to keep breathing myself into it; and finally to dear Zach, for reminding me daily that Grace is real and that feeling good is natural.

Divine Openings has shown me beyond doubt that there is no subtraction in the universe; every person and each experience expands us and all of Creation. For everyone who has added to my life and to the sweet completeness of this moment, thank you.

Table of Contents

Opening Invitation	4
Introduction	6
One: Slow Down And Show Up	11
Two: Make All Feelings Good	33
Three: Take It To The Presence	55
Four: Go With The Flow	69
Five: Choose Your Focus	81
Six: Just Say Yes	95
Seven: Get Yourself To The Party	115
Eight: Drop The Story And Feel The Feeling	139
Nine: Take Time To Align	155
Ten: Be Happy Now	167
Closing Invitation	179
Quotation References	180
Instrument Panel	181
About Melinda, Testimonials	183

Opening Invitation

"God, what am I going to do?"

I didn't plan the words. I didn't have a close relationship with God. They came in a flash of unusual clarity and from stark honesty and acceptance of what was absolutely true at that moment: I desperately wanted another drink, and I knew that if I had one I would surely continue to suffer, or worse. At that moment, both drinking and not drinking were unimaginable and equally unbearable.

In that conscious blink of an impossible choice, I surrendered. I gave up.

"God, what am I going to do?"

In my absence, Grace rushed in. It was immediate. I was blanketed by a sense of relief and the knowing that all was well. My breath deepened, my body relaxed and I was filled with a pervasive sense of gratitude. I knew the battle was over. My desire to drink was lifted right then.

This spontaneous gift of Grace changed my life. It left me without doubt that there was something bigger than me that was personal too—that somehow knew my heart and cared about me and my well-being. And it filled me with certainty that I was worthy to receive its blessings.

I knew it was a gift, and my deeply-felt gratitude kept it alive for many years and kept me well-planted in The Presence, where, I've since learned, Grace truly lives and breathes.

It's only when I started taking it for granted that I began, slowly, to fall back under the spell of old habits and the forgetful confines of mind. Choice by unconscious choice I turned away from the cherished present and found myself back in crisis more than a dozen years later. Grace hadn't abandoned me, I had simply become too weighted down with "what I think" and "how it is" and "what's possible" (and not) for Grace to lift me into its realm of possibility.

So, when I discovered Divine Openings in 2009 I recognized the profound blessing of what was being offered. Before, Grace had come without understanding of how and, more importantly, how not to squander it. Now, mystery was replaced by the possibility of mastery; I was offered the Grace and its operating instructions—a clear and precise map that has since proven reliable, when I use it. I clung to it as if my life depended on it, which it probably did.

Because I tend to complicate things, I made Divine Openings simple for myself. Whenever I remembered I asked: *"Am I really here right now? Yes or No?"*

The question itself, this conscious pause in the action, already indicated an opening of awareness and invited me to go deeper still into The Presence—to choose *Yes* as fully as I could. When I accepted the invitation and really showed up—and I didn't always—the path ahead naturally came into focus. From this choice, others became available:

I could stay locked in my head, or I could open to the experience of my body. I could hold my breath, or I could breathe. I could avoid my feelings, or I could feel. I could complain or I could look for things to appreciate. I could make my experience wrong, or I could find ways to make it right. I could focus on what I didn't want, or I could turn towards what I did.

When I was present, I could choose to push against and resist, or I could choose to soften and accept. I could choose to react, or I could choose to wait, align, and respond. I could choose a course that didn't feel good, or I could choose one that did. I could choose to hold onto the belief that I was alone and on my own in this moment, or I could choose to let go and experience that I wasn't.

Ultimately—I could make choices that opened me to Grace, or I could make choices that didn't.

I didn't have choices when I wasn't awake and aware. So really, the choice was: am I willing to be present in my life—or not? If I wanted my freedom, and I did, the choice was obvious: *Yes*.

I don't know how, but Grace undeniably flows through Divine Openings. What I discovered is that whenever I am willing to show up for whatever is happening, Grace flows more easily, and Grace then makes subsequent better-feeling, forward-facing choices easier to make.

Within a year of beginning Divine Openings, Grace made it *easy* for me to once again embrace sobriety. As well, an acute, life-threatening illness gently slipped into remission. The accompanying relief and the clear, certain knowing that Grace was truly present and available *to me personally* allowed me to fully relax again for the first time in years. Nothing in my life was untouched by this gift. Grace just made everything easier.

Today I have new habits. Grace softens me and I make consistently better feeling choices for myself. Many of the "issues" and "problems" I'd worked on for ages now lift right out of my life, as if by magic; the lighter my touch and the less I strive, the easier they move.

Part of the magic, I've learned, is in not seeing things as "issues" and "problems" anymore. Divine Openings has turned me around so I no longer focus on things I don't want. I'm finally facing towards what I want—*with* the Flow of Life, in the direction of "Ah, that feels better..." For Grace to pour in, I just had to be willing to stay out of my own way. It was really that easy.

There is still plenty of mystery in Grace. What's no longer mysterious is how to stay open to its flow. Divine Openings gives me the ability to keep my Grace connection alive. The choice is always mine and my choice is always **now:** am I willing to pause, breathe, soften, allow, feel, accept, appreciate, celebrate, and show up for my life?

Are you?

Introduction

In 2006, Lola Jones spent twenty-one days in complete silence and emerged with a gift of Grace that activates awakening, ends suffering, and dramatically changes lives. For three weeks she let go of everything and opened fully to the Mystery within, communing only with The Presence. She committed to *feel* everything unconditionally, and as emotional energy was allowed to move, she expanded naturally into alignment with her Divine Self. Divine Openings was birthed from this experience.

Things Are Going Great In My Absence; How To Let Go And Let The Divine Do The Heavy Lifting chronicles Lola's awakening and, by Grace, also awakens the Pure Life Force in you. The book helps you understand what to expect in your unfolding and gives you the conscious-mind tools to let it be easy.

Grace and ease are the hallmarks of Divine Openings. Grace is a gift that cannot be earned, so working on yourself or trying to make yourself worthy of it denies Grace by definition. Letting your encounters with Divine Openings be relaxed and playful allows Grace to flow more freely.

And so this is not a workbook. Instead, it's a *Playbook*—a hands-on, play-along companion to *Things Are Going Great In My Absence* that will help you more deeply embody its teachings and enhance their practical value in your daily life. It's your personal training manual!

In this *Playbook* you will engage even more deeply with what you read in *Things Are Going Great In My Absence*. Additional activities and fresh ways of experiencing the material will light up new parts of your brain, increasing integration and assimilation. This will occur naturally as you show up and play.

Years before her twenty-one days of silence, Lola Jones made a decision to stop the incessant seeking and spiritual work and discover instead an enlightenment path of ease and joy. She chose to stop relying on outer guidance and reclaim the sanctity of her own inner guidance. Divine Openings is the extraordinary result of these clear, unwavering decisions.

Lola's goal—and mine—is for you to reconnect with your own Divine guidance and quickly step into your own power. Can you let it be fun and easy, as intended?

Divine Openings is simple and Lola's voice is strong and clear. Nevertheless, unworthiness, self-doubt and my own addiction to seeking and spiritual work initially deafened me to the possibilities of Grace and ease. I literally could not conceive of the reality she offered and found every opportunity to complicate, confuse and weaken her message. I had built up significant momentum behind the equation:

(Hard Work + Suffering) x Time = Eventual Freedom and Enlightenment

Despite increasing evidence that disproved my math, it still took some time for my mind to accept the simplicity of Lola's, where Grace does 90% of the work and my 10% is mainly staying awake and learning to let it. But when I used her equation, the positive, practical results in my everyday life multiplied in amazing and unexpected ways. Could it really be this easy?

I was motivated to find out. Despite my resistance, I also had a strong desire to feel better, and I made a decision to do what was suggested.

So I showed up and I practiced thinking and feeling in new ways, to the best of my ability. When I did, I noticed that I felt better, and each little bit of relief made it easier for me to soften and allow Grace to flow more freely. Soon I began experiencing the new reality I'd been unable to conceive of.

After two years of Divine Openings my life was greatly transformed. Addictions had fallen away, significant health and financial crises had turned around, and a sometimes-debilitating pattern of depression had lifted. Three years after that, I was the first to graduate from the Guide Certification Program. And two years later, I am one of a select group of Guides listed in the Directory on the official Divine Openings website, have been made a mentor in the Certification Program and am privileged to be the author of this *Playbook*. I am privileged because it was my own deepest desire to write this book.

I could never have imagined any of these things when I happened upon Lola's book in May 2009, nor could I have imagined feeling as at home in this world, and in my own body, as I do today. But I felt that I had found something exceptionally special. Divine Openings is special. If you feel this too, then you are in the right place.

Lola's power and intention flow through these pages, filtered through my voice and experience as someone well acquainted with the ways our small selves can complicate, confuse or try to sabotage waking up. Although I came to Divine Openings having had profound experiences of awakening, my overall, default vibration was quite low and I never could sustain the higher elevations.

My mind—a good, strong, logical mind—had learned well from other minds around me; it had learned that the world wasn't particularly safe but that if it stayed one step ahead of the game, it could protect me. "One step ahead" meant constantly anticipating problems, fears and worries, and my mind kept me well-supplied in these. "One step ahead" meant being in control, and my mind always had a plan to fix the fears, worries and problems it supplied. "One step ahead" also meant frequently not being in the present moment—where, I've since learned, real safety and solutions come from.

Always being one step ahead meant I didn't meet life directly very often. And because feelings live in the present moment, it meant I didn't actually *feel* very often either. I thought I was feeling, but mostly I was rehashing stories or mentally trying to understand, figure out, process, fix and protect myself from what I was feeling. I avoided things that felt too big (a lot of things felt big to me) and unwittingly created and tethered myself to a big old pile of ignored-messy-scary-stuff which yanked me back to earth after every vibrational trip to the Mountain Top. I was on the same emotional roller coaster many of you may be on.

If I wanted off the ride, I needed to take a step back and become willing to pause. And I needed to learn how to feel. To do this, I needed the cooperation of my mind. This wasn't a particularly easy process for me, but along the way I've learned a lot that I know can help everyone who has a mind—especially people with beautiful strong minds.

Through Divine Openings, my mind has finally accepted that life moves easier and feels better when it's not running the show. Nothing has been more enjoyable and empowering than deliberately moving into my body and truly embodying my life. Coming back to earth, paradoxically, has opened me to consistently higher altitudes—and helped me sustain them. This is what I hope for you too.

The Grace that flows in Divine Openings is the engine that powers your awakening. Increasingly, your Large Self will be in the driver's seat. It's important, however, to not just get your small self on board with this new arrangement but to offer it ways to enjoy the ride!

To that end, in this book I focus on the essential ideas and practices that I think build a solid foundation for expansion, including how to soothe your mind so that it can understand, support and hopefully come to enjoy and appreciate your unfolding. I don't incorporate everything in Lola's book, but you have ample opportunity to integrate the information, experience *and* vibration I do. Repetition is intended!

Ultimately, you are being invited to really claim and step into your 10%. As you get absolutely clear about what your 10% is, it will become easier to let go and let The Divine do its part.

I encourage you to play with the material! Have fun and move through it at your own pace. It is strongly recommended you read the book front to back, as with *Things Are Going Great In My Absence*, but if you are called to dip a toe in here and there, then do that. Trust yourself. Enjoy the ease that will become your new norm.

Structurally, the *Playbook* is divided into ten sections, coinciding with the implied structure of *Things Are Going Great In My Absence* where material is punctuated by ten Divine Openings. Each of these ten *Playbook* sections is organized around a broad theme that emerges from and corresponds to the material in Lola's book. Though Lola does not designate and name the ten parts of her book as I have, I present material in the same basic order that she does, organized in a different format designed to give your brain new and fresh ways to absorb, assimilate and step into your understanding and power.

Ultimately the words and activities in both books are signposts, pointing to experiences the mind cannot wholly grasp and understand. Don't confuse the words with what they are pointing you towards. They are not *it;* you don't *need* the words. As long as you stay open to Grace, you will learn what you need as you go along. The words simply help keep your mind happy, engaged and out of the way so that you *can* stay open to Grace!

So take them in, fill yourself with their possibility, appreciate them, then let go and go live. Give the words time and space to come alive in your life. Life provides endless opportunities to apply what you've read and experience what the words are really pointing to. Let it!

Divine Openings works. I believe that everyone who wants to experience its magic can deepen their fulfillment with the help of this *Playbook*.

IMPORTANT: This book is *not* a substitution for *Things Are Going Great In My Absence*. It augments it and helps you deepen into the ideas and experiences there. Only *Things Are Going Great In My Absence* gives you the enlightenment initiation. It is the foundation for your awakening and must be read in full and in order, ***slowly*** and with presence. **Your presence increases its value to you.** The same is true for this *Playbook*. Discover the joy of reading slowly, deeply and purposefully.

Neither is this book a substitute for the Divine Openings Level 1 Online Course (nor is Level 1 a substitute for this book). The Level 1 Course and this *Playbook* both offer foundational support for people new to Divine Openings or for anyone wanting to deepen their understanding and experience of its essential teachings. But they are purposefully different in emphasis, content, and style.

The message of Divine Openings is quite simple, but most of us have had common sense and simple truth trained out of us. In my own experience, it was necessary to hear the message countless ways, a hundred different times, before my small self got it enough to get on board—or at least to stop resisting so much!

This makes sense vibrationally. The words—and the experiences they point to—have a clear, high vibration. From lower vibrations (where many of us begin), it can be hard to really hear them. The vibrational distance is too great, and it's clogged with emotional "interference" that makes clear reception difficult.

But as you keep showing up, interference dissolves and the signal gets clearer. *Your* vibration rises, moving you ever-closer to the signal itself. From higher vibrations, the words progressively come alive and you are able to embody their invitations more easily. Eventually you simply experience the joy, peace, and relief from struggle and suffering that you may have been seeking for years, or even decades. At this point the words become unnecessary—you live from the knowing, empowered perspective that all is well and that life does flow in directions you intend, when you let it.

In the beginning, however, words are helpful. Fortunately, there are a lot of them in Divine Openings! Reading Lola's books, playing with the Online Courses (which include a large library of audio and video recordings), and amusing yourself with this *Playbook* soften and relax the mind, giving it fun and interesting things to do while Grace does the heavy lifting. The words *and* vibration in all these various platforms encourage the small self to get to the party while easing it out of the driver's seat and coaxing its foot off the brakes.

Enjoy the ride!

*"Divine Openings opens you up so you can let in the Grace
that always is and always was raining down on you.
It simply reveals to you what was already there and who you already are."*
Lola Jones

Section One: Slow Down And Show Up

Savor The Possibilities

Divine Openings is not like other programs you may have tried. From the beginning it is essential to be clear about what Divine Openings is and is not: it is not a do-it-yourself program; it is a relax-and-let-it-be-done one. Grace does 90% of it for you. You get everything you need—the Grace and the know-how to keep it flowing.

The reality that Divine Openings points to is very different from the reality most of us were raised and taught to believe in. Make time at the start to absorb what is being offered. Its truth and depth will expand with time, but the clearer you are from the start, the easier it will be to let in. Turn from what hasn't worked in the past and focus instead on what is possible here, now.

⏸ PAUSE AND REFLECT on What IS Possible

Throughout the Playbook, *these opportunities to* PAUSE AND REFLECT *provide fertile soil for your deepening and expansion. Write, scribble, doodle, draw, paint, collage and create in the space provided here. Or, take your reflections off the page and into your body and sing, chant, dance and move them into life. Take time and make space for the new ideas and vibrations to take root.*

In the very beginning of *Things Are Going Great In My Absence* (pages four and five), Lola Jones beautifully describes what Divine Openings can do for you. Did you take it in?

- Read it again, right now, with presence and purpose: open your mind to the fresh ideas.
- Soon enough you will have proof that all this and more is possible. For now, savor the possibilities. Invite them in and give them space to grow. They will!

▶ PLAY ALONG: Begin Your List Of Possibilities

Divine Openings is a practical program that can change the course of your everyday life. These PLAY ALONG *activities invite you to bring the concepts to life. You can't think your way through Divine Openings. But neither should you work at it. The activities in this book are meant to be fun! If you show up for them with curiosity and willingness, you will increasingly embody their practical wisdom and your expansion will naturally unfold.*

Things Are Going Great In My Absence has dozens of descriptions of what Divine Openings is and does. List them here! As you read or experience new ones, add to your list and refer back to it when you need reminders about what is possible and clarity about where you're headed. Better yet: change Lola's pronouns from "you" to "I," "me," "my" and "mine." Own the possibilities! **(All quotes in this *Playbook* are from the 2016 10th Anniversary Edition of *Things Are Going Great In My Absence*.)**

- *"Divine Openings increases my capacity to tap into direct knowing."* (Lola Jones, page 11.)
- *"Divine Openings doesn't work on details at all. It doesn't need to because it works at the meta-level (very big picture) and causes quantum evolutionary leaps at every level of my being simultaneously."* (Page 24.)

*"The experience of unfolding is the real adventure.
Slow down and enjoy every single moment!"*
Lola Jones

▶ *PLAY ALONG: Be Willing To Start Where You Are*

It's hard to get where you want if you don't know and accept where you're starting from. That's like trying to get from Boston to New York when you believe you're starting in San Antonio!

- There is a copy of the Instrument Panel at the end of this book. Note where you currently are in each of the important areas of your life (health, wealth, family, friends, work, creativity, adventure, general wellbeing…). Date it for future reference.
- There's no wrong starting place; you can get anywhere from here if you know where here is!
- Now ask, "What do I currently believe is possible in these various areas of my life?"
- If you keep showing up, your belief in what's possible will change and grow. Note where you are now and then check back later to celebrate what has changed and revel in your expansion!

If you are not yet familiar with the Instrument Panel, dig right in to the best of your ability and then circle back as you learn more. Expansion is never a linear process; your understanding and experience are forever deepening! It's entirely possible to accept where you are and know more is coming.

▶ *PLAY ALONG: Make A Commitment To Yourself*

Create a special setting to make the following commitment formal and special. Light a candle, kneel at the altar of your favorite tree, or simply close your eyes, relax your shoulders and breathe. What you do is less important than how you do it. Take time to align with your willingness and intent. When willingness is sincere and intention is clear, Grace can't help but flow.

- I am willing to believe that Grace is real. I can call it what I want (Love, Life, Oneness, God, Buddha, Allah, The Divine…) as long as I am willing to believe it exists.
- I am willing to let Grace flow in my life.
- I don't have to know how it works for Grace to flow, but it helps to understand that Grace flows easiest when I get out of the way and *let it*.
- I am willing to let go, get out of the way, and let The Divine do the heavy lifting.

Slow Down

The first few sections in *Things Are Going Great In My Absence* contain foundational information for your mind and important vibrational preparation for the experience of Divine Openings. If you are used to rushing through material and gobbling up information, make a different decision here. Read not with the goal of collecting more knowledge but with the intention of being guided to your own inner Source of knowing; that knowledge is fresh and timely in every moment.

Slow down. Allow the vibration of what you are reading to penetrate and absorb into every atom of your body. Keep in mind that bodies and emotions, words and thoughts—physical *and* Non-Physical things—are all made from the very same energetic "stuff," just vibrating at different speeds. As you

"Talking, reading, and hearing about spiritual things are often barriers to actual inner knowing. But you're about to have a direct experience of The Divine within you. This invisible Larger aspect of You will soon become a normal everyday part of your life."

Lola Jones

read, this vibrational soup mixes, merges and interacts to create new inner pathways and possibilities in you. Unless you utterly resist, you naturally move towards vibrational resonance with the words, but it happens more easily, quickly and enjoyably with your unhurried awareness and participation.

Divine Openings gives what you've wanted all along: *direct experience* of The Divine. Direct experience is not a mental activity. It happens beyond the mind and initially, your mind may feel threatened. It may come up with many reasons to hold onto what it knows and continue doing what it's done. It may try to convince you that it gets all of this already! The mind doesn't like change and will do what it feels it must to avoid the unique experience of Divine Openings.

The conscious-mind teachings in *Things Are Going Great In My Absence* retrain your mind to get out of the way and help it understand what is happening vibrationally. They soothe and guide it as it moves out of its comfort zone. This training is an essential part of Divine Openings.

And, beyond the words and teachings, your mind also relaxes from simply spending time in higher vibrations—from reading Lola's books, perusing the website, and playing here. So much happens in the absence of the part of us that needs to understand, control, and make things happen!

So, as you play in the arena of words, focus on your *experience*; read with your whole being, not simply your head. Allow the words to settle into your body. Breathe them in, fully and patiently. Don't grasp: if you try to figure out or work at this, you'll slow your progress. Touch lightly, go slow, and have fun. When you're relaxed you are more porous to Grace and assimilation happens more easily.

⏸ PAUSE AND REFLECT on *The Absurdity Of "Working On Yourself"*

You're encouraged often here, and in *Things Are Going Great In My Absence*, not to not work at this. And, more than almost anything else, the old paradigm of seeking, striving and working on one's self can be difficult for people to release. But working on yourself delays your enlightenment indefinitely. It activates an endless conveyer belt of things to fix and keeps you trapped by a belief that you are incomplete now and have to earn or work for your freedom and peace. Grace will show you otherwise, but Grace, like enlightenment, must be allowed; you don't earn Grace! Barriers to Grace fall away when you decide to let go of seeking and working on yourself. You *can* experience now what you've been seeking, without all the work.

- Pause and really absorb the fact that working on yourself postpones your freedom. When your conscious mind truly gets this, your awakening (and Grace!) flows much more easily.
- How has past seeking prevented you from actually getting there? Recall other modalities, religions or systems of "self-improvement" you've practiced and inquire if they've added to the belief that you can't possibly step into a new reality without suffering, undo sacrifice, and unending repair and penance. Don't make them wrong; just feel the momentum behind the beliefs.
- Your beliefs create your reality. In the reality you are creating now, do you want to be seeking enlightenment or experiencing it?

*"You will learn to use your Free Will wisely, but it isn't work, it's just paying attention.
There's no 'working on yourself' or 'processing' in Divine Openings.
You just stay awake."*
Lola Jones

▶ *PLAY ALONG: Investigate How "Working On Problems" Feels*
Divine Openings invites you out of the old, problem-focused, "have to fix this in order to get to that" reality and into a new paradigm where you get to simply create what you want starting now.

- Is there an area of your life you've been working on for a long time?
- How do you feel when you think about it? Is your body relaxed? Are you able to breathe deeply? Or do you feel constricted and tight?
- Now shift your focus from the "problem" to what it is you want. If you can, experience your pure desire, without focusing on its current lack or needing to know *how* it might come to be.
- When you focus on the "problem," where are you on the Instrument Panel? When you focus on what you want, where are you?
- Describe how each perspective feels in your body. Which feels better?

▶ *PLAY ALONG: Slow Down And Notice What You Notice*
Reading about spiritual concepts is not the same as experiencing them in the same way that reading about a delicious meal is not the same as actually tasting it.

- When you eat today, intend to slow down and show up for the experience. Use all your senses to notice the textures, colors, flavors and smells.
- Actually taste what you are eating. Be present as you move the food to your mouth. Feel the power in your jaws as you chew. Get curious about your tongue, your lips, and your breath.
- Notice how you feel about what you're eating. (This is important!)
- Don't make this into a chore; just intend to notice a bit more than you ordinarily would.
- How did it feel? Where were you on the Instrument Panel? Even if you noticed you felt *irritated* or *impatient,* that's awareness! Without awareness you can't choose differently, so celebrate moments of awareness!

Note: Throughout this book I often italicize specific Instrument Panel readings (like *irritation* and *impatience*) in order to emphasize and reinforce this new language of emotion and vibration. Please note too that I offer just one of many ways you could be feeling at any time. Feel what's true for you!

What Do You Want?
Divine Openings offers a practical spiritual enlightenment; you have a body and live in the physical world, so money, health, fun, adventure and relationships are important. Your experience right now, good or bad, is creating desire—either desire for more of the same or desire for change. When not contradicted, desire creates what comes next in your life, because true, unresisted desire naturally inspires willingness and intention. When these things are aligned, your life flows in the direction you want. Divine Openings shows you how to stay in alignment. The first step is acknowledging where you are and what you want.

"The Presence, of which you are an integral part, does want you to have what you want in the material world, so the more you can get out of the way and let that in, the easier it can be delivered."

Lola Jones

◐ **PLAY ALONG: Identify Where You Are (And How Far You've Come!)**
The following inventory is reprinted from the Divine Openings website. It helps clarify where you are now and where you want to go. If you've been in Divine Openings for a while, you can also use it to clarity how far you've come! Use one color to circle the answer that best shows where you started, then another to show where you are now. If you're new, simply indicate where you are now. In six months, when you take the inventory again in another color ink, it will be hard for the wrong-seeking, miracle-denying mind to dispute that Divine Openings works!

On a scale of 1 to 10, circle where you are NOW on each item.
Ten (10) is for "I'm 100% there, it couldn't be better."
One (1) is for "I'm far from where I'd like to be on this item."

- Today's date (a momentous date!) __6/13/17__
- Happy and fulfilled 1 2 3 4 5 6 7 (8) (9) 10
- Have profoundly intimate experiences of my Higher Power 1 2 3 4 5 6 (7) 8 9 10
- Have deep, intimate, caring, friendly, responsive relationship with God 1 2 3 4 5 6 7 8 9 10
- Have a quiet mind 1 2 3 4 (5) (6) 7 8 9 10
- Have low stress (1) (2) 3 4 5 6 7 8 9 10
- Have little anxiety 1 2 3 4 5 6 7 (8) (9) 10
- Am at peace 1 2 3 4 5 6 7 (8) 9 10
- Have let go of grudges, blame, anything weighing me down 1 2 3 4 5 6 7 8 9 (10)
- Have let go of being a victim, taken advantage of, or abused 1 2 3 4 5 6 7 8 9 (10)
- Go deep quickly in meditation 1 2 3 4 5 6 7 8 (9) 10
- Routinely have profound spiritual insights 1 2 3 4 5 6 7 8 9 (10)
- Am intuitive and guided clearly from within 1 2 3 4 5 6 7 8 9 (10)
- Understand my guidance, dreams, and signs I get 1 2 3 4 5 6 7 8 9 (10)
- Family issues are few 1 2 3 4 5 6 7 8 9 (10)
- Stale or broken relationships are easily renewed 1 2 3 4 5 6 7 8 9 (10)
- Have great relationships 1 2 3 4 5 6 7 (8) (9) 10
- Have lots of love in my life 1 2 3 4 5 6 7 8 9 (10)
- Have an ideal romantic relationship 1 2 3 4 5 6 7 (8) 9 10
- Have great friendships 1 2 3 4 5 6 7 8 9 (10)
- Have self-confidence and self-love 1 2 3 4 5 6 7 (8) 9 10
- Feel worthy of good things 1 2 3 4 5 6 7 8 (9) 10
- Am free of the illusions of "reality" 1 2 3 4 5 6 7 8 (9) 10
- Am free of the bondage of money 1 2 3 4 5 6 7 8 (9) 10
- Money is a non-issue in my life 1 2 3 4 5 6 7 8 (9) 10
- I play the money game successfully 1 2 3 4 5 6 7 8 (9) 10
- I let money come to me 1 2 3 4 5 6 7 8 (9) 10
- Am efficient, I get a lot done with time left for play 1 2 3 4 5 6 (7) 8 9 10
- Am creative and innovative 1 2 3 4 5 6 7 8 9 (10)
- Have made peace with age, mortality, and time 1 2 3 4 5 6 7 8 (9) 10
- Am master of my world, I'm creating it consciously 1 2 3 4 5 6 7 (8) (9) 10
- Am loving and compassionate 1 2 3 4 5 6 (7) (8) 9 10
- Am the person I want to be 1 2 3 4 5 6 7 (8) 9 10
- Have freedom from fears (of anything) 1 2 3 4 5 (6) (7) 8 9 10
- Change negative patterns without hard work or processing 1 2 3 4 (5) (6) 7 8 9 10
- Find it easy to cease bad habits 1 2 3 4 5 6 7 8 (9) 10

Life offers endless possibilities,
all unfolding from where you are, right now.

- Am addiction-free (food, drug, drink, shopping, gambling, sex, other) 1 2 3 4 5 6 7 8 9 **(10)**
- Have stopped seeking and no longer toil and work on myself 1 2 3 4 5 6 **(7)** 8 9 10
- Enjoy every day 1 2 3 4 5 6 **(7)** 8 9 10
- Laugh and smile a lot 1 2 3 4 5 6 **(7)** 8 9 10
- Have fun, light-hearted play 1 2 3 **(4)** 5 6 7 8 9 10
- Attract good things into my life easily and naturally 1 2 3 4 5 6 7 8 **(9)** 10
- Am in control of my mind and emotions 1 2 3 4 5 6 7 **(8)** 9 10
- Smooth out my emotions easily 1 2 3 4 5 6 7 8 **(9)** 10
- Feel good most of the time 1 2 3 4 5 6 **(7)** 8 9 10
- Am free of depression, sadness 1 2 3 4 5 6 7 **(8)** 9 10
- Am doing my true soul's desires 1 2 3 4 5 6 7 **(8 9)** 10
- Have a high level of ease in creating 1 2 3 4 5 6 7 **(8)** 9 10
- Am really good at manifesting what I want 1 2 3 4 5 6 7 **(8)** 9 10
- Am making a living at something I enjoy 1 2 3 4 5 6 7 8 **(9)** 10
- Am working for joy as well as to make a living 1 2 3 4 5 6 7 8 **(9 10)**
- Tap into my innate genius easily 1 2 3 4 5 6 7 8 9 **(10)**
- Am living my heart's desires 1 2 3 4 5 6 7 **(8 9)** 10
- Things happen for me quickly 1 2 3 4 5 6 7 **(8)** 9 10
- Am productive and focused 1 2 3 4 5 6 **(7 8)** 9 10
- Connect with others, communicate more effectively 1 2 3 4 5 6 **(7 8 9)** 10
- Am at ease in my job, work relationships, leadership 1 2 3 4 5 6 7 **(8 9)** 10
- Am making a big difference in the world and for others 1 2 3 4 5 6 7 8 9 **(10)**
- Am inspiring others to a better life 1 2 3 4 5 6 7 8 9 **(10)**
- Feel physically great and healthy 1 2 3 4 5 **(6 7)** 8 9 10
- Have energy and stamina 1 2 3 4 5 **(6 7)** 8 9 10
- Am in shape and at ideal weight 1 **(2 3)** 4 5 6 7 8 9 10
- Feel and act young 1 **(2 3)** 4 5 6 7 8 9 10
- Have a genuinely positive attitude 1 2 3 4 5 6 7 8 **(9)** 10
- Feel good emotionally and mentally 1 2 3 4 5 6 7 **(8 9)** 10
- Bounce back from setbacks fast 1 2 3 4 5 6 7 **(8 9)** 10

How do I want to experience my life differently?

In what other areas would I like to have major breakthroughs, shifts, or increased ease and freedom?

What is my main intention for doing Divine Openings?

"The desire to do what I do now was born when I first laid eyes on an enlightened master, my first teacher, in 1985. 'But get real,' I told myself, 'you can never be what he is.' My secret dream, too unbelievable to share with anyone, was to write a book that could change people's lives, even in my absence."

Lola Jones

⏸ *PAUSE AND REFLECT on Daring To Dream*

Many people are afraid to acknowledge and ask for what they want. They might feel unworthy of it, think it's not practical, believe it's impossible, or despair that they have to earn it or figure out how to make it happen.

- Where do you hold back from fully feeling your desires and wholeheartedly wanting what you want? As you reflect, notice how holding back feels in your body. Feel the *No* embodied by "can't," "couldn't possibly," "shouldn't," or simply, "not me."
- Now reflect on something you truly do want and notice how that feels in your body.
- If there is *hope, excitement* or perhaps a feeling of inner expansion, this shows you are vibrationally aligned with your desire. If there is *fear, pessimism* or a sense of inner tension and contraction, this shows you are not aligned vibrationally with what you want.
- You are not being asked to do anything yet. For now you are being asked to simply notice how different beliefs, assumptions, thoughts, emotions and desires feel in your body. Later, you will be given specific techniques that enable you to more easily align with and move towards the things you want.

▶ *PLAY ALONG: Say Yes!*

Yes opens you to Grace and helps realign your focus, intention and power so you consciously work with Life rather than against it. It gets you pointed forward, towards what you want. *Yes* raises your vibration and returns you to sanity and clarity. *Yes* is a choice that can transform your life. It's a habit that gets easier with Divine Openings.

- Focus gently on one area in your life where you've wanted and asked for improvement.
- Now, soften your focus and see if you can daydream your way towards *Yes*. Let go of any old stories and relax into the energetic expansion *Yes* brings. Even a slight movement in that direction can feel better now and open pathways between you and what you want. Have fun!
- If the mind jumps to how it will happen, let go: give it to The Presence on a deep exhalation of *YES*. Let go and let The Divine do the heavy lifting! Your job is to savor the swell of energy that always accompanies *Yes*.
- Intend to say *Yes* more often! There's almost always a *Yes* to be found in any situation.
- Listen to music that excites your *Yes*. Accept the invitation to step into its vibration! Or better yet, dance yourself into it!
- Say *Yes* out loud to at least ten things right now! Really do it!

Waking Up To A New World

In *The Wizard of Oz* Dorothy goes to sleep in a black and white world and awakens to a new set of rules and Technicolor possibility. In this new world she and her friends eventually remember their innate authority to do and have what they want—by remembering and being who they were all along.

"Most of the world thinks that if they had more money (for example),
things would go better, and then they could be happy.
But that's backwards. That's 'have, do, be.' The reverse is true;
if you could 'be' happier and more centered, you would 'do' better, and then you'd 'have' more money.
This book is not going to ask you to 'do' anything different.
You'll allow your true inner being to emerge until you are being your Large Self,
then you'll watch your actions and thoughts flow naturally from that.
Then your life and circumstances will shift around to fit who you newly are.
They must, and they will, without effort."
Lola Jones

Divine Opening awakens you to such world. As you adjust to life in the higher altitudes (over the rainbow!), you recognize that it's the old rules that were backwards.

In the old world, *doing* and *having* certain things (often with unnecessary personal struggle and sacrifice) were believed to be prerequisite for *feeling* and *being* certain ways. In your new world, Divine Openings makes it easier to think, feel and be—or vibrate—the way you want to be, and then the things you want to do and have come more easily. External circumstances always reflect internal ones, so managing your inner vibration becomes the most effective way to create change in the outer world. You attract change rather than working for it. Divine Openings gives you a foolproof set of instructions (and the boost of Grace) to help you do this.

This is a huge paradigm shift, but as you move through *Things Are Going Great In My Absence* and, by intention and Grace, as you naturally begin to live more from the states of being you desire—living more as your expanded, unlimited, Non-Physical Self—belief in the rigidity of physical world "reality" softens. You recognize its ever-shifting, malleable nature and understand that the process of creation is much different, and easier, than you thought.

When you looked to him for guidance, the "man behind the curtain" led you astray because he didn't know any better. You didn't either. Now you do. This is a new day. Start fresh! Like Dorothy, you've always had the power to go Home. You reclaim this power when you remember that it's not about doing or having anything different; it's about acknowledging, embracing, being and experiencing exactly who you are, right now—perfect now *and* eternally expanding.

⏸ *PAUSE AND REFLECT on States Of Being*

When you concentrate of states of being, Life more easily bends to your desire.

- Is there a *having* or *doing* that you want? What is the true state of *being* that you desire from having or doing this thing?
- Perhaps you want more money. Can you identify a deeper desire? What would it really give you? A feeling of *worthiness* or accomplishment? More *freedom, ease* or *joy*? A sense of *safety* and more *security*? (Security and safety are not on the Instrument Panel Lola has created: where would you plot them on yours?)
- Are there other things in your life that provide the same feeling? Can you remember other times you felt that way? Can you *be* that way now?
- Use your imagination to immerse yourself in those experiences and turn up the volume on that particular feeling right now! The more time you spend in this vibration, the easier it is for money to come to you.

⏸ *PAUSE AND REFLECT on Just Driving Away*

"Just drive away" is a powerful mantra from the book, but you may not have applied it specifically to your life. It's a good reminder for when you may be giving external circumstances too much power.

Once upon a time a brave soul took back her power...

- Are there currently areas in your life where you feel stuck in traffic, your foot on the brakes, getting more and more *angry, frustrated* or *impatient*? Do you tend to be a honker?
- Focusing on and pushing against outer resistance just gives it more power.
- How can you change the scenery a bit, to soften your resistance and feel better now? Where could you "just drive away?"
- Turn away from unwanted things when you can.

▶ PLAY ALONG: Write A New Hero's Story

"We're proud of our struggles and suffering. We make heroes of those who were lost and then found, as any movie plot demonstrates. Struggle is highly valued and rewarded." (Lola Jones, page 22.)

- Do you have a personal "hero's story?" Describe it here.
- Now, consider that the adversities you have boldly and so courageously struggled against… may largely exist *as a result* of your struggling.
- Life absolutely is sometimes hard. But (and this can be tricky to understand at first) you could just as easily create your life with fewer struggles.
- You **are** a creative being. What you create depends on your focus. Ask: "Am I focused on problems and struggle or am I focused on solutions and possibilities?" You get to choose.
- Eyes forward, with NO judgment about what's been, what new possibilities could open up if you started telling a new story—one that feels better?
- Energetically, how can you allow your perspective to expand and shift direction towards increased *empowerment* (which is high on the Instrument Panel)? Anything that moves you in that direction will feel better, and when you feel better, you are more effective in the world.
- Write yourself a new hero's story! "Once upon a time a brave soul took back her power…"
- Begin to notice what fresh inspiration arises to help with current challenges as you reclaim power to create with greater joyfulness and ease.
- Ripple the vibration of this possibility out into the collective!

Support for Your New Vibration

As you begin to click your heels and wake up to your True Nature, the people back in Kansas may not understand or support you. Ancient Mind keeps people in the drama of survival and lack, and the pull of Ancient Mind is strong. Our world worships hard work, suffering, and struggle and commonly disparages those who don't buy into their version of reality. Fortunately, Grace is softening the pull of Ancient Mind on you. As it does, do not waste your energy pushing against consensus reality. The world around you will shift as you shift. Let the world be.

Attend instead to your own experience. To get the most from Divine Openings, you'll need to fiercely protect and manage your focus and attention. It's too easy to unwittingly give power away to someone else's reality.

*"Those of us living the Divine Openings life
belong to a collective consciousness
that exists beyond Earth's consensus reality,
and we celebrate, support, and uplift each other
in our explosion into bright new possibilities."*
Lola Jones

If you need help, know where to find it. Look within, first: your Large Self is always there to offer love, support and the most appropriate, timely guidance. If you decide that you need or simply want outside help—and we all do sometimes—the Divine Openings community provides support and understanding for whatever you might be going through. They've been there! You can enjoy the Member Forum when you're a member of any Online Course. By enrolling in the Level 1 Self-Paced Online Course, you give yourself a solid Divine Openings foundation—with countless hours of audio and video to keep you immersed in the new, higher vibration. You can also get support in private sessions and small group calls, and get soothing at any time from simply visiting the website.

⏸ PAUSE AND REFLECT on Supporting Yourself By Reclaiming Power

Consider the ways you give power away. Do you allow the media to determine how you feel about the economy or your overall level of security? Do you let your doctors decide how healthy you are? Parents, bosses, children, friends and lovers all have a point of view. You forfeit power when you blindly concede, but you also leak power when you push against their well-meaning but vibrationally disempowering thoughts and suggestions. Learn to find your truth, and then occupy it.

- Notice how it feels when you stand your ground, firmly, but without defense. Notice how walls between you and the world crumble when you meet it this way.
- Practice standing this way. Feel that sweet, sacred spot where *I Am* meets *You Are*, without attack, defense or resistance.
- Draw, doodle or write about how this experience feels. Plot it on the Instrument Panel.

▶ PLAY ALONG: Experience Support At Any Time

Many people have never experienced true, consistent support. But support is always available.

- Your Large Self loves and supports you infinitely and eternally. Give yourself the gift of deepening into that relationship! It's as close as your breath, your heartbeat, and your *Yes* to what is, here and now. Discover this truth.
- Perhaps the next time you are awake at three o'clock in the morning you can consciously intend to experience what being supported feels like. Start by feeling the bed under you.
- On a purely physical level, you are always supported by the Earth. Stand and walk with the intention of viscerally experiencing this support.
- Have you ever felt supported by the water? While in the air?! I have!
- Deepen your relationship with all the ways you are truly supported. Look for and celebrate evidence of support! They are everywhere.

▶ PLAY ALONG: Support Yourself With New Habits

Rather than having "issues," consider you've developed habits that no longer serve. You don't need to fix anything, you just need to create new habits, especially in regard to movement and stillness.

Let busyness be an invitation
to slow down and show up.
"Here, now...here, now...here now..."
As you meet yourself in this moment,
your experience naturally expands.

- Vibration is energy and as your vibration rises, energy needs to move. If you don't have a lot of physical movement in your life, support yourself by finding ways to move. This is vital!
- For fun, take a walk and intend to be awake and present. Turn off your music and tune into your body. Look down (this moves you into your body), relax your shoulders, and lead with your heart. Inhabit your whole being, not just your head.
- Attend to Life flowing through you. Consciously inhabit the place where your legs meet your hips; notice how your breath quickens, slows and moves; feel your shoulders, neck and arms. Get curious about how it feels to be supported by the ground.
- Get moving, but also be willing to slow down, show up and simply feel. For most, especially in the beginning, daily communion with The Presence supports this new way of being.

Section One Mantra: Slow Down And Show Up

GRACE IN ACTION

Each of this Playbook's *ten sections ends with a mantra and an invitation to relax into deeper communion with what has been explored there. These* GRACE IN ACTION *pieces are meant to speak directly to the part of you that remembers—and give that part an opportunity to lay down roots and spread its wings. The intent is to engage your heart, draw you into direct experience, and create a softening that makes it easier for Grace to enter.*

You are walking in your neighborhood. Though your feet are on the ground, you are not here.

Unexpectedly, the smell of summer jasmine catches your attention. Or perhaps it's a feeling of sadness, the stir of wind across your face, or the weight of a child's hand in yours that breaks your trance and beckons you back, now.

You could ignore the invitation; often you do. But something has nudged you awake, and in this moment you feel more alive. There's an awareness that wasn't here before. You choose to pay closer attention.

As you meet yourself in this moment, your experience naturally expands. There is a swelling, an opening in your chest, a feeling of greater wellbeing, a dropping of mind/thought. You feel more alert, present and connected.

Awareness has woken up, opening a space between you and your habitual reactions. New possibilities have exploded into life. Who you are just got bigger. Rest here.

*"Emotional mastery is prerequisite to enlightenment.
No amount of esoteric knowledge can substitute.
It's possible to have flashes of profound illumination
but lose it when confronted with emotional or challenging life situations.
Paradoxically, when you can be with any feeling, you will feel good most of the time,
and it helps sustain your enlightenment."*
Lola Jones

Section Two: Make All Feelings Good

Your Continuum Of Being

The human experience occurs on a continuum. Lola uses the terms "small self" and "Large Self" to describe the range of experience on that continuum. Small self *"is simply that more narrowly focused, less knowing aspect of us that thinks it is separate from God, other people, and Nature; the part that resists the Grace that would carry us with ease"* (Lola Jones, page 27), whereas Large Self experiences no separation from any part of Creation, never judges anything as "bad" or "wrong," and is always aligned with Grace. Small self isn't less spiritual or worthy than the Large Self, it just has its own essential part to play in your life and in your awakening.

Your small self never feels quite as good as the Larger part of you that's always blissful and knows all is well. The worse the small self feels, the greater out of alignment you are with your more expanded Large Self. It's supposed to feel bad when you are out of alignment so that you *know* you are out of alignment and are therefore motivated to make choices that point you back towards greater alignment!

Ideally, you experience something that doesn't feel great and think, "Oh, this is a message showing me that I'm experiencing this situation MUCH DIFFERENTLY than my Large Self is." Then you go about finding ways to think and feel that are more in alignment with your Large Self—in ways that feel *better*—and as you do, the outer situation shifts in response (or your perception of it shifts). Sometimes this happens quickly, sometimes it's gradual. As you move up the Instrument Panel, outer shifts happen more easily and quickly. No matter what happens out there, however, you feel better because you are a little more aligned with the part of you that always feels good!

Unfortunately, rather than embracing the feeling/message as an opportunity and invitation to turn towards our Large Self, most of us believe that feeling "bad" means something is wrong— that we've done something wrong to feel that way, or that the feeling itself is wrong, or that it points to something wrong in the world. But judging things as wrong moves us further away from our Large Self, who never judges. And judgment is like glue; it sticks us to what we're judging and makes it much harder for us to actually move in a direction that feels better.

When you judge and make things wrong, there's always a belief that you cannot feel better until the wrong thing gets fixed. But judging and making things wrong literally fixes things in place and prevents them from moving in a better-feeling direction. They create resistance, and "what you resist, persists." This isn't just some trite cliché. *Judging and making things wrong keep them stuck.*

The small self naturally refines if you don't judge and resist it, just as feelings (and Life) naturally move in a better feeling direction when you allow them to. Everything in life wants to move, and the natural momentum of this movement is always in a better feeling direction, towards the experience of the Large Self. Your job is to stop swimming *against* the current! Divine Openings shows you how. As Grace eases resistance, you regain the power to choose your focus and reclaim your place *with* the Flow. You learn how to make things right again!

Resisting unwanted aspects of yourself only strengthens them. What you resist persists.
Just watch them come and go, observe them as energies, and embrace them all.
Awareness is all you need to over time become more your authentic core self."
Lola Jones

⏸ PAUSE AND REFLECT on *Being Your Large Self*

The *bliss* and *joy* of Large Self is not entirely unknown to anyone. We've all had "peak experiences" and moments of being "in the Flow."

- Recall moments when you naturally expanded into alignment with your Large Self—when everything simply opened up and you just knew that all was right with the world.
- What was happening at the time? Were you worried, closed off and working at something you didn't enjoy?
- Or were you happy, open and at ease, doing something you loved and that felt good?

⏸ PAUSE AND REFLECT on *The Power Of Acceptance*

Divine Openings offers a map to deliberately take you back to the freedom of your Large Self. As with any map, you must be willing to begin where you are. You may not necessarily like where you are, but accepting where you are helps nudge your vibration in the direction of "I feel better." It's the paradoxical, magical, miraculous alchemy that happens when this, right now, is met with allowing.

- What if you didn't judge or interpret your experience but instead met your life directly?
- What if you met each moment not needing to fix or change it but willing to simply allow, feel, and experience it?
- What if "why is this happening" and "what does it mean" didn't matter? In the moment, they don't. Understanding can't take you through; it comes in hindsight, from the other side.
- Your full participation with this now moment is what gives it its divinity and moves you in a better feeling direction.
- The Presence is the now-moment not judged, resisted, avoided or denied but wholly met and embraced. In The Presence you commune with The Presence—with you own Large Self.
- This communion offers the fulfillment you really seek.

▶ PLAY ALONG: *Relax And Feel Into The Presence*

What happens when you meet yourself in The Presence?

- What are you feeling right now? Don't answer with words: answer by first noticing what you feel in your body.
- Notice your seat on the chair, your feet on the ground, your hands holding this book. Let awareness sink into your body. Be in the experience you are having. Give yourself time to fully arrive.
- Then, perhaps inquire if there is a general mental or emotional atmosphere, or vibration, that you are aware of. You don't necessarily have to label it, but it's important to begin checking in, often, and noticing that you are always feeling and experiencing *something*.
- Let the vibration live in your body and just notice how it feels.
- Pause, breathe, and notice the spacious, expansive nature of direct experience.

*"When you can move emotional energy, you can move any energy.
Manifesting is literally the ability to focus and flow energy."*
Lola Jones

PLAY ALONG: Stop Fixing Yourself!

Contrary to what you've probably been told in the past, the small self does not need to be fixed, healed, cleared, worked on or processed. Energy simply needs to move, and when it does, not only do you feel better now but the small self begins to evolve, naturally. Divine Openings helps with this. If you are still working on yourself or trying to avoid or fix unwelcome thoughts, feelings and inner states rather than acknowledging and being with them, you are actually keeping in place the very things you're desperately trying to get rid of.

- Make a decision right now to stop!
- If the small self needs a project to replace "working on itself," intend that it get on board and remember to pause, often, and breathe, relax, be aware, notice beauty, feel, play, accept, enjoy, smile, appreciate, look for evidence of Grace, and commune with the eternal Presence of Large Self.
- Small self loves projects, so give it ones that are useful!

❖

Emotions Are Meant To Move

Emotions, like all kinds of energy, are meant to flow. When emotional energy isn't allowed to freely move, problems develop. Difficult and unwanted life experiences show you where emotional energy is moving slowly or not at all. They indicate places you've ignored feelings or made them wrong and haven't let energy move. We all do this, to greater or lesser degrees, so please don't heap more judgment on your resistance and blame yourself for not being better at feeling! Most of us never learned how to truly let emotional energy move. Today is a fresh start; celebrate that instead!

All emotions are part of the same stream of Divine energy, just vibrating at different speeds. The better feeling emotions are vibrating faster than those that don't feel as good, but all of them are important. Emotions let you know your proximity to your Large Self. When you're flying high in *appreciation* or *joy*, you are more aligned with the Larger part of you that lives up in those altitudes than when you're grounded in *fear, powerlessness* or *depression*. Ongoing, habitual lower Instrument Panel readings indicate that your engine is filled with stagnant old gunk you've avoided feeling. It's a perfect feedback system as long as you don't think you have to heal, process or clean out the sludge!

You don't! To get from "grounded" to "flying high" you simply have to let feelings move. Emotional energy quickens and rises naturally when not resisted, and when it does, you feel better and create better feeling outcomes. Emotions you avoid, resist and don't feel are nevertheless still vibrating, and they eventually play out in your life in ways you may not like. When you are willing instead to feel and let these vibrations move, they don't have to materialize in the physical world to get your attention!

More and more, you will appreciate that it is Non-Physical energy that primarily creates in the physical world. As you practice moving emotional energy, you will begin to see shifts in your outer world. As you become more adept at this, you'll learn how to deliberately create what you want in the physical world. Further on in *Things Are Going Great In My Absence* you will receive specific tools and coaching to help you become a master at moving emotional energy and creating more deliberately.

*"Too many spiritual people try to avoid lower emotions, magically transcend them,
make them go away with sessions or modalities, or deny them.
They want to avoid any 'bad' lower emotions and leap straight up into higher ones.
I call that a 'spiritual bypass.' Interestingly, spiritual development is stunted
until you deal with the very human realm of emotions.
Enlightenment requires fully embracing the whole human experience,
fully embodying in the physical—not rising above it or escaping it.
As enlightened humans, we're bringing Heaven to Earth,
not looking for a fast pass out of here."*
Lola Jones

⏸ PAUSE AND REFLECT on Spiritual Bypass

A spiritual bypass happens when you make any feeling wrong, bad, or "unspiritual" and skip over it by avoiding, denying or resisting feeling it. Feelings are neither good nor bad. They're all just bits of energy vibrating at different speeds, showing you how you are vibrating in relation to your Large Self. The less you judge them, the easier it is to allow all the various bits to rise in vibration and move you into greater agreement with your Large Self.

- When your smoke alarm goes off, loud and annoying, do you make it bad and unplug it? When the gas gauge reads empty, unfortunate as it is, do you make it wrong and ignore it?
- What feelings have you made wrong? Are there feelings your family decided were wrong? Your friends? Your teachers, clergy or culture?
- If you're not sure, look at your life and pay attention to your habits of feeling and experience.
- A while ago I recognized that a pattern of lifelong anxiety had deep roots in *overwhelm* and *impatience* and seemed to reflect a belief in the scarcity of time. Even though I had an abundance of time relative to most people, my *experience* felt perpetually squeezed and rushed.
- In a single moment of presence and clarity I suddenly got that impatience and overwhelm weren't indications that something was wrong; they were simply Instrument Panel readings—vibrations that needed to move.
- I saw how I'd made the feelings wrong and had also made myself wrong for having them—heaping more "bad" on already not-great feelings. It's no wonder I'd avoided feeling them and had instead rushed around trying to fix things in the outside world, obsessively rushing to cross things off my to-do list!
- But focusing on and managing things *out there* added to my avoidance of what was true *in here*—that I had a backlog of unfelt, stagnant emotion that was keeping the vibration alive.
- With new awareness, great curiosity and strong intention, I decided to not make the feelings or myself wrong and instead celebrate the opportunity to embrace and move them.
- I focused on my inner experience rather than the outer events that seemed to trigger them, and within days I could feel this old, crusty vibration begin to soften, move and lift.
- On the other side, I notice that I don't nearly experience the world through that particular lens to the degree I once did. And because I was willing to pause and be with myself in those moments rather than bypass and rush into action, I developed a new relationship with time. There's no scarcity in The Presence, and increasingly this has become my experience too.
- Now, when impatience and overwhelm do come up—as they will, as normal responses to life events—they move easily because the huge backlog of bypassed, resisted and unfelt emotion and vibration has moved.
- There's great power to reclaim when you start noticing emotional territory you've ignored and bypassed. When you reclaim each of your Instrument Panel readings, they become familiar waypoints on the map; you still sometimes stop—because life happens—but you now know that they are just part of the journey. You know where you're headed, how to stay pointed in that direction, and you get waylaid less and less.
- When you don't make any feeling wrong, you quickly start moving again in the direction you want.

*"Each Divine Opening pre-programs the emergence and eventual dissolution
of old energies, patterns, and habits that no longer serve you.
It points up the old small-self density that is not you,
the fearful illusion and pain your mind created,
and it all rises in vibration as it is fully felt.
Again: if you don't resist it, pain doesn't become suffering."*

Lola Jones

⏸ PAUSE AND REFLECT on Trusting The Flow

We naturally want to hold on to feelings and experiences that feel good. But holding on shows that we don't trust that more will come, and the outer reality reflects this expectation. Your fullest, non-resistant participation in any moment expands your enjoyment and raises your vibration, and from a higher vibration, you attract more feelings and experiences that feel good. You begin to trust that more will come when you let go and experience that more does come!

- A moment is like a breath: to fully let in the next one, you must completely let go of the current one. Take a breath now.
- When you let go and exhale, do you doubt that the next inhalation will follow?
- What if you could trust in Life the way you trust in your own breath?
- How can you celebrate each "ahhh" and "aha!" and enjoy them fully without holding on too tightly?

▶ PLAY ALONG: Begin To Notice Non-Physical Energy

Everything is birthed in the Non-Physical. Assumptions, beliefs, thoughts, feelings and intentions determine vibration and your vibration determines what happens in the physical world.

- What happened in your world today? Did events match your expectations? They generally do, although Grace is always looking for ways to bring you more than you expect.
- Write about a specific example of life matching an expectation.
- Develop a habit of noticing how Life may be reflecting your beliefs and expectations of it.
- Just notice. There's no need to force change. If change is wanted it will flow easiest from awareness of what is and a new, light-as-a-feather intention.
- *Everything* is birthed in the Non-Physical.

A Divine Opening Gets Emotional Energy Moving

There are ten Divine Openings in *Things Are Going Great In My Absence*. A Divine Opening awakens you *with* pure Energy/Light/Intelligence *to* pure Energy/Light/Intelligence. It introduces a very high vibration into your field and all that is not in resonance with it begins to shake loose. Old, stuck, resisted and unfelt feelings finally get the opportunity to rise in vibration, and you get lighter as your vibration rises. Enlightenment is this lightening up into your natural state.

A Divine Opening is not a healing or energy work and it doesn't fix anything. It simply creates space for things to move and opens you to the Larger experience of who you really are.

After your first Divine Opening emotional energy will begin to move. Grace helps things move fast! It's up to you whether this will be painful or not. If you resist the movement, it's likely that you will struggle and suffer. But suffering is optional.

*"When you decide to awaken, you're asking Grace to raise your vibration,
and as that happens lower vibrational energies activate
and begin to move upward rapidly, often en masse.
Maybe in the past you'd get stuck in the lower feelings,
but with the Grace-assist of Divine Openings, they move quickly
(unless you seriously resist them).
We are deeply brainwashed that we have to learn by suffering,
but if you can let go of that, suffering isn't necessary at all.
Just feel your feelings and let them move.
If you don't try to fix the feeling or make it go away,
and don't make it wrong, you won't suffer.
Resistance turns mere pain into suffering."*

Lola Jones

Developing a new relationship with your feelings (your 10%) is the cornerstone of Divine Openings and a subject we'll visit again and again. For now, however, if you have a habit of running from feelings that don't feel good, remind yourself that avoiding feelings keeps them alive. Soothe yourself by understanding that that movement is good. Know that as old, deeply embedded vibrations are allowed to move, barriers to experiencing your Large Self are crumbling. Keep your eye on where you are headed. Decide not to resist your resistance!

Always, you can ask The Presence for help. The best help to ask for is always a lessening of resistance so that what needs to flow can.

⏸ *PAUSE AND REFLECT on the Vibratory Nature Of Life*

Everything in Creation is energy made manifest by way of vibration, pulsing at different speeds. Physical and Non-Physical "stuff" all have distinct energetic signatures, determined by vibratory speed. Emotionally, you feel better when energy is vibrating at a higher speed. When you let energy move, its vibration quickens and rises. Your whole human experience is determined by your vibration so understanding what vibration is and how to manage it is essential.

- Start to think of emotions in terms of energy and vibration.
- Understanding emotions as vibrational energy can make it easier not to get swept away in their stories. Focusing on the how's, what's, when's and why's of an emotion keeps it in place. Recognizing and feeling the *vibration* allows it to move.
- When you are feeling *afraid* or *sad,* consider that your vibration is rather low and slow. When you are *happy* and *excited,* notice that it's higher and faster.
- Begin to pay attention to how these different vibrations feel in your body. Don't judge, just notice. True, unbiased awareness helps things move!

⏸ *PAUSE AND REFLECT on Opening Your Pipes*

Divine Openings opens your pipes so more Grace can flow through. Visualize and feel the incredible power and potential of this gift:

- Imagine a water pipe filled with thick, gooey gunk. It's stagnant and clogged. Scarcely a dribble can pass through the blockage.
- Imagine now that something begins to shake things up; a high, fine vibration is introduced into the system and all the billions of stagnant, clogged particles begin to quiver and pulse. As they do, space between them is created and in this opening, movement is now possible.
- Because they have space to move, those billions of atoms can now vibrate at an even faster speed until critical mass is reached and *whoosh*—they vibrate themselves into a new state altogether; the solid mass softens and liquefies. It can now flow easily through the pipes.
- As well, the pipes are now more open so that everything can move through much easier!
- Divine Openings has already introduced a high, fine vibration into your system. *Whoosh!*

Feelings are like weather;
they're sometimes unwanted or inconvenient,
but they're not wrong,
and you're not wrong for having them,
just as the Earth isn't wrong for having weather.

▶ PLAY ALONG: Soften, Allow And Align

This cannot be repeated enough in the beginning: You may be used to thinking that lower emotions point to something wrong "out there" and therefore focus, mistakenly, on the physical "problem," hoping you can solve it and therefore "fix" the feeling.

But really, the feeling itself IS what's trying to get your attention! You feel bad because you are not aligned, or in agreement with, your Large Self, to greater or lesser extents, depending where you are on the Instrument Panel. The feeling isn't wrong and doesn't need fixing: it's giving you vital information about where you are and how to move in another direction. When you soften, feel and accept it, you allow it to move and begin to close the perceived gap between you and your Large Self. Then outer-world things you thought the feelings were about can shift more easily, reflecting this greater inner alignment.

Divine Openings stirs up old, resisted emotions so they can move and rise. Let them! You will feel better when they do.

- In what areas are not-so-great feelings indicating that you are not aligned with your Large Self, on that subject? Is there one particular area (money? health? relationships?) where your Instrument Panel reading is well below the *ease* and *empowerment* your Large Self feels about it?
- When you attend to your feelings instead of circumstances they seemingly result from, you find relief quicker.
- So, if you are feeling *fear*, perhaps, instead of focusing on what you're afraid of, gently allow the fear to be there.
- If you start to get sucked into the story of what you think the fear is about, remind yourself that your current fear is really just indicating a place that you momentarily feel separate from your Large Self. In this case, you feel so separate that you are feeling frightened and alone.
- Feel the fear instead; you will find it in your body. Allow it to be and it will begin to move.
- As it does, it will pull you in its wake—*whoosh*—towards your Large Self. From that increased alignment you will feel better and have greater resources to handle the outer circumstances.
- Relief is a sign that you have stopped pushing against some unwanted experience or feeling. Feel the relief in allowing!

▶ PLAY ALONG: Soften To Let Go And Let In

Saying "soften" to yourself, often and gently, helps you let go. It also makes it easier to let in Grace.

- Close your eyes and scan your body. Notice any places that might be tight, clenched or gripped. Take your time. Feel into your belly, your shoulders, your hands, jaw and breath. These are common areas where people tense and tighten without even knowing it.
- Now, bring gentle, soothing, soft attention to any areas of physical tension or holding (places in your body where you've forgotten how to let go). Meet yourself where you are. Don't try to change what is, just be with it. Soften.
- When you soften, allow and relax, space opens up. Do you feel it? *More space = more Grace!*

*"Feelings of unworthiness are one of the biggest blocks to receiving Divine Grace,
so the sooner you can release those judgments against yourself,
the more fully you can receive the good that is flowing to you and through you all the time.
Unworthiness is a lie and a mistake. Let it go. Decide you are worthy right now! God already has.
Why not agree and get back in alignment with The All That Is?"*

Lola Jones

You Are Worthy

You exist so you are worthy. There is nothing to do; you do not need to prove your worthiness to God or man. If you were born, you are worthy.

You did not feel unworthy when you were born. Unworthiness is something you picked up along the way.

A vibration of unworthiness can block or slow the flow of Grace to a trickle. You just cannot let it in if you don't feel worthy to accept it.

If you feel unworthy, you will live the consequences of your belief.

It is possible to step into your worthiness, here and now. The Presence within knows and experiences its absolute worth. Each time you meet yourself there, you are pulled into that knowing vibration. (Locate *knowing* on the Instrument Panel.)

Intend to claim your worthiness!

❚❚ *PAUSE AND REFLECT on Worthiness*

Your Large Self does not feel one iota of unworthiness, and at times of greatest connection, communion and alignment, unworthiness doesn't exist for you. Unworthiness has no objective reality: it is a mental construct—a learned, vibrational habit. It hums inside you at a very low, slow and decidedly not-good-feeling frequency. When you dip within earshot, you hear its protest; when your vibration soars, you do not.

- Most people feel different degrees of worthiness in different areas of their lives.
- In which areas do you feel more worthy? Do you feel worthy of a large paycheck but not a fulfilling relationship? Of having a strong, healthy body but not a supportive group of friends?
- Bring awareness to habitual patterns of *un*worthiness and notice that they are just that: habits and indicators of vibration. Welcome and acknowledge the indicators; don't make them wrong but don't buy into their version of reality either.
- Instead, feel and allow the vibration of unworthiness to rise and move. As it does, you will experience that *what remains is worthiness*.
- Worthiness is your natural state. Claim and allow yourself to receive what's already there.

▶ *PLAY ALONG: Feel the Vibration Of Worthiness*

Worthiness and unworthiness are vibrations you feel in your body.

- Think of an area where you feel worthy to have, do and be what you want.
- Stand, now, and feel yourself into that sense of worthiness. Let it ripple through your body. Feel the strength in your legs, the power in your arms, the fullness of your breath, and the

"This moment is all there really is. This book is about being happy in this moment, and when you are happy in this moment, you are in agreement with The Presence. The time for enlightenment is NOW. The time for mankind to wake up is NOW. The methods are right here for you, right NOW, in this book. You are NOW on your way to enlightenment. Really! Finally."

Lola Jones

certainty in your stance. Embody your worth and memorize the vibration. Don't just think about this, do it!
- Now think of an area where you do *not* feel worthy to have, do or be what you want.
- Move your body into this experience of unworthiness. Is your body opened or closed, contracted or relaxed? Just notice.
- What happens if you move your body into the worthiness *stance* when you are not feeling particularly worthy? Does it shift your vibration towards worthiness? Play, practice, notice.

❖

THIS Is Your Moment
"All your power is right here, in the present moment. All you need to know is available here and now." (Lola Jones, page 22.)

When you really get this, you get that you don't need more experience, knowledge, healing or fixing to awaken and be happier right now. Truly, you didn't even *need* whatever experience or knowledge got you to the crossroads of this moment, although it's all unfolding perfectly. Every moment is entirely new and fresh. All possibilities exist now. You can blast off from anywhere.

If you think you need more _____ (fill in the blank: modalities, time, knowledge, ability, etc.) or that whatever you need isn't available now, you delay yourself indefinitely from getting what you want. If you think you have to fix what's broken before you get "there," you can spend a lifetime trying to fix yourself and you still won't arrive. You are not broken. You are simply experiencing certain feelings and situations as entirely appropriate vibrational responses to your life thus far.

If there are places you want to evolve, the opportunities will present themselves in the right moment. If you stay awake, don't avoid or resist what your life is reflecting to you, and trust that this moment is a perfect launching pad for everything you want, you'll grow. Grace will assist. Grace is almost tangible when you really relax into this moment, into The Presence.

 PAUSE AND REFLECT on Waiting With Presence
When you come into the present moment, you commune directly with Life—unlimited, ever-inclusive, and forever-expanding. Any moment expands when it is occupied fully; so does your own inner space, providing fertile ground for greater clarity and possibility. Life offers up its treasures the more you live from this space of pure potential.

- For some, waiting for what's next becomes another way to avoid what's happening now.
- If this feels true for you, ask: "What am I waiting for?"
- Then ask: "What if I could experience that now?"
- Maybe you can't immediately *do* or *have* everything you want at this moment, but right now, while you're waiting, you can practice *being* who you want to be when those things show up!
- In every moment, you get to choose your focus.

Intend to find peace within the unfolding.
Intend to find comfort within the mystery.

- Begin to notice how you fill your time when you are waiting. Pumping gas, waiting in line or stuck in traffic, you can remain on mental autopilot or you can intend to wake up, look around, notice what surrounds you, choose your focus, and occupy your experience now.

⏸ *PAUSE AND REFLECT on Tuning To The Frequency Of Now*

Your experience is like a radio dial. You have certain preset stations that are specific to you at this time and space—certain practiced vibrations you attune to most often. But in truth, there is a wide range of possible stations/vibrations that you can always tune into right now. Divine Openings makes it easier to tune into stations that are higher on the vibrational dial, ones that broadcast more harmonious frequencies.

- As you begin to experience moments and periods of higher vibration, pause and take note.
- Feel the vibrations in your body and begin to learn and memorize them!
- Expand your repertoire of high-vibe "presets" so you can consciously tune in when you need a lift.
- At the top of the dial, on a continuous loop, your Large Self hums an adoring, beguiling melody. Can you hear it? Can you feel it? Even if you can't—it's always playing, even now.
- What will life be like when you can easily find *that* station on your dial, whenever you choose?

▶ *PLAY ALONG: Choose Ease*

You can awaken with ease. Create a soothing, beautiful space—both inside and out—and purposefully decide to:

- Expand through joy. You learn and grow much easier through joy than through suffering.
- Keep it simple. Don't muddy your vibration by mixing Divine Openings with other modalities. More is not better.
- Value all your feelings. No feeling is wrong; each is a perfect messenger that you need to hear right now. They provide your guidance system. Acknowledge and appreciate this guidance!
- Claim your worthiness. Claim the gifts that are yours! Claim what Grace showers on you.
- Intend to let go of addictions. Addictions are painful. They limit your power and choices. But it is entirely possible to let go of any addiction with less pain and struggle than you might currently believe. Savor this possibility, relax if you can, and *allow* desire, willingness and the intention for freedom to grow. Grace will respond to these invitations. If you need help imagining a new possibility and support stepping into one, by all means get it! Ideally, the support you receive should feel good.

Making these choices at this moment is perfect for you. Your mind may insist that this moment is far from perfect and judge that you "should" be further along or generally someplace other than here, now. Your mind cannot grasp that all is well now *and* you want more. This can only be experienced. Divine Openings helps you experience the truth of this extraordinary paradox.

Are you large enough to welcome every experience? You are.

Section Two Mantra: Make All Feelings Good

GRACE IN ACTION
The loudest voice is often the hardest to hear, especially if it's been screaming at you your whole life.

For many of us, the constant hum of "I shouldn't be feeling this way" has become part of our normal, accepted background noise. It's the ubiquitous guard at the gate, and we don't even recognize our captivity. "I shouldn't be feeling this way" keeps anger rock hard, sorrow from softening, and shame from experiencing the love and connection it needs. It says we need to change but denies us the way.

"I shouldn't be feeling" keeps us stuck in hopelessness and powerlessness. It stops us at the holy threshold of *Yes,* and by blocking the way through, it condemns us to no way out.

Are you large enough to welcome every experience? You are. Do you have what it takes to face the guard at the gate? You do. Are you willing, this one time, to ignore its voice?

Will you allow your bad mood, and your despair, and your fear and frustration and anger, worry, and doubt?

Will you accept your habits of manipulation, and control, and judgment, jealousy and blame—even as you choose, perhaps, not to act on them?

They all are part of you, awaiting and needing your allowing and your acceptance so they can fulfill their purpose and help you move 'morewards'—towards more—eternally.

Will you open your heart to them, take them in, honor their need, and feed them your *Yes*? Will you grant them their freedom?

If you do, they will grant you yours.

*"There is much more to you than you see,
yet it's not always so easy for you to be sure of that
since you use your physical senses to decide what's real
and your physical senses cannot always perceive the Non-Physical you.
But your Large Self—that vast, unlimited, Non-Physical aspect of you
of which you are but a small physical aspect—is always there for you."*
Lola Jones

Section Three: Take It To The Presence

There's More To You Than Meets The Eye

Divine Openings awakens you to the Non-Physical aspect of yourself that can't be perceived through the physical senses. This Larger experience of Self is what you return to when you die, but Divine Openings helps you experience it while in a physical body.

You are not *all* that God is, but you are a focal point for God to express through. Your Large Self is a more focused, personal aspect of God that created and cares about you individually. *You* are the dynamic interplay between this Large and even more narrowly-focused small self. There are no actual boundaries between any parts of Creation; how Life experiences itself is really just a matter of focus, and your focus can expand (and contract) at any time.

From its greater perspective, your Large Self can provide guidance, possibilities and solutions that your small self cannot access. As you bring awareness to this expanded aspect of yourself, you begin to experience life more and more as your Large Self. This alignment is what you have been seeking.

⏸ *PAUSE AND REFLECT on The Call Of Your Large Self*

The Larger part of you knows that all is well no matter what may be happening in your life and emanates a homing signal so you can know this too. This signal echoes through anything that inspires or helps you to feel better than you are currently feeling. Truly, anything can be an invitation to turn in a better feeling direction. When you turn towards a thought, emotion or action that feels better than what you are currently thinking, feeling or doing, you turn in the direction of your Large Self. When you consistently turn in that direction, you expand into a Large-Self perspective and begin to experience that all truly is well.

- Is there an area in your life now where all is well? Feel into that. Turn up the volume! Savor that high, fine vibration until it permeates every cell of your body.
- Better yet, make a new habit to begin your day that way! Your Large Self knows that all is well, so take time before you get out of bed to feel into this knowing, as best as you're able from the vibration you're in. Soften into The Presence and gently reach for that expansion. You'll feel it when you do.
- Starting the day on this high, fine wave is deliciously *empowering* (way UP on the Instrument Panel)! Sometimes you'll feel light enough for Life to literally carry you. Those will be days when everything flows.

▶ *PLAY ALONG: Meet Yourself Here, Now*

Wherever you are at any moment offers the perfect opportunity to expand into greater alignment with your Large Self. Your Large Self always meets you exactly where you are. The question is: are you willing to show up?

"What a concept—that God behaves according to our expectations and is actually willing to do what we want rather than dictating its will to us!"
Lola Jones

- Pause right now and deepen into this moment. Take a slow, conscious breath (or two). Notice what you notice, starting with your body. Feel the substance of you.
- Like soaking a sponge with water, saturate yourself completely with molecules of awareness.
- As you soften and make space for yourself, notice what fills the space. Don't hurry. Be there.
- Perhaps a feeling has emerged that you don't want to feel—*fear, sadness, anger* or *frustration*. Inquire if you feel *impatient* to move on to the next section. Maybe you think there's something "there" that isn't available "here."
- Whatever you might be feeling, intend to recognize its vibrational nature. Impatience, fear, sadness, anger and frustration each have a particular vibration. When you focus on vibration rather than the specific *story* about what you are feeling, it begins to move—which is what energy is supposed to do (and why it feels bad when it doesn't).
- One of the best ways to help vibration move is to get out of the way and let Grace do it for you.
- You are invited to close this book for the rest of the day and go live your life! Notice if this feels difficult. If it is, that's okay. You can tolerate the discomfort. Feel it and let it rise. Claim your freedom!

God Is An Experience, Not A Concept

In India, Lola learned two new names for God, translated as: *One who does as is bidden* and *One who is at the beck and call of the devotee* (Lola Jones, page 49). These descriptions suggest that God has no self-nature and can only be known through your experience. Your experience is determined by what you expect and allow God to be.

Concepts and second-hand experiences of God limit your experience. If you start fresh, throw out old concepts and beliefs, and intend for a close-up, tangible relationship with God, you will find the freedom, peace and fulfillment you've been seeking.

You may never be able to put your experience into words or describe it to another. That's okay; words limit. The experience itself and how you feel is always more real and powerful than ideas and descriptions and what you think.

❚❚ *PAUSE AND REFLECT on The Unlimited Nature Of God*

"We rob ourselves of infinite possibilities by holding onto limiting concepts of God." (Lola Jones, page 49.)

- Before designing your relationship with The Divine, take time to truly absorb these words.
- How might life unfold differently if you trusted in both the unlimited *and* personal nature of God?
- How could everything change if you really believed God wanted for you what you want for yourself—and more??
- Can you daydream yourself into that vibration and feel it in your body?

"The Divine will be whatever you want."
Lola Jones

▶ PLAY ALONG: Communicate With God

Your Large Self knows that it is an aspect of God. In other words, a part of you hasn't ever forgotten who you really are and what is possible for you.

- Imagine your Large Self welcoming you to Earth on the day of your birth. What would it most want you to remember? What guidance might it offer? How would it speak to you?
- Write yourself a "Welcome to Earth" letter from this Large-Self perspective.
- Your Large Self is always communicating with you. Ponder and appreciate all the ways your Large Self can and does "speak" with you on a daily basis.
- Communication is a two-way street. How do you respond? Do you make time to pause, listen, and really hear? How do you feel when you do?

Create Your Own Experience With God

Now you get to design your own personal relationship with God. The truth is, you already have. You are just being invited to do it consciously, with new awareness, perhaps, about the nature of God—which is to be at *your* beck and call.

When you create a real, up-close and personal connection with The Presence within, you naturally expand in that direction, as if a magnetic force is attracting you (it is). If you make it *the* primary relationship in your life, you transform in ways you cannot imagine. As you experience the peace and power of alignment with your Large Self, your life starts changing in often astonishing ways. You lose any doubt that your Large Self wants for you what you want for you as you realize your Large Self IS you. Your greatest desires are satisfied through this communion. Eventually, miracles become commonplace.

It is worth your time to question what beliefs you hold about God and deliberately let go of ones that do not excite, lift and expand you. You are always the only limiting factor in your experience of God, so intend to let go of the barriers that have kept you from experiencing your unlimited, blissful nature!

⏸ PAUSE AND REFLECT on Your Current Beliefs About God

Consider the beliefs you currently hold about God—what God is, what God does, how God behaves towards you, and what God wants for you.

- Be honest about what you think and believe now, and draw, write, move, sing and otherwise embody your current perception.
- How does it feel? As you reflect, does your body feel open, expanded and *joyful*? Or does it feel heavy, contracted, *ashamed, judged* or *afraid*?
- Awareness brings greater choice and allows for new possibilities. Notice what you feel, but don't judge! Things move easier when you don't make them wrong.

*"The Indweller does not judge what you choose to do with your gift of Life
but gives Free Will to all, knowing there is no ultimate risk for an eternal being.
Mistakes don't exist either, and are not tallied by The Divine nor held against you.
Karma is a primitive religious concept, much like Hell.
They both deny Grace, and you can let go of them now.
Each life, each day, each moment, is a fresh new start."*
Lola Jones

⏸ PAUSE AND REFLECT that The Divine Does Not Judge You

Many people move through life with a pervasive sense that they are *wrong*. This inner voice of judgment and shame can be so ingrained that it escapes detection (this is an example of a "blindspot"). For some, this omnipotent, omnipresent voice is attributed to God, consciously or not. This puts enormous distance between them and The Divine.

- Your Large Self does not judge you or your actions. It's always there, inviting you into greater alignment and expansion, but it never sees where you are, what you do or who you are as wrong. As you move into increased agreement with your Large Self, neither do you.
- This isn't an agreement you can reason your way into. Instead, intend it, gently and softly. Pause often and ask, "What does my Large Self think about this?" and then let yourself receive the answer. To receive, you must make space to allow something new to enter.
- If you are currently quite low on the Instrument Panel, the answer you receive might not be good news. If this is the case, please, *please* try to remember: this is NOT the voice of your Large Self! The vibrational distance between you may be too great for you to hear the good news your Large Self always has to share.
- Intend to bounce off any "bad" news you get and know that as you progress up the Instrument Panel, good news becomes easier to hear. Just as the sun is always shining above the clouds, so too is the eternal good news of your Large Self.
- Imagine how fantastic it will feel when you burst through the clouds and discover that the sun was there all along!

▶ PLAY ALONG: Design (And Savor) Your Relationship With The Divine

Now you get to design your own personal relationship with God. What do you want?

- Which qualities are important to you? Humor, playfulness, compassion, support?
- Do you want an authority figure or a relationship that feels more like a partnership?
- What states of being do you want to experience? *Acceptance, courage, love, empowerment...?*
- As best as you're able, feel into the experience you want. If you want to feel supported, feel the ever-present support of the ground under your feet. If you want to feel cherished, imagine yourself as a tiny baby and feel your own love for that cherished, precious child.
- There's no right or wrong relationship; there's only what feels good to you, at this time. The relationship will change as your vibration rises, so it will be in constant evolution! For now, be as specific as you can and hold nothing back.
- All relationships flourish with focus, care and attention. God is always there; it's up to you to attend to and nurture the connection. As you show up for this relationship, God will show up in your life.
- Bring everything to The Presence—your fears, your worries, your joys, and your sorrows. Talk with God like you would a friend, lover or confidant. Ask for what you need. Open yourself to its unlimited love and guidance. Offer your own love and appreciation.
- Write, draw, dance or sing this new relationship into being!

"At the bottom of everything is bliss. At your core is bliss.
This is no surprise once you realize that your Large Self experiences only bliss.
When you're experiencing something less, you're just not fully in alignment with your Large Self.
You've wandered off course and gotten separated from the Oneness, the Flow of Life.
Soon you'll know how to get back home easily."
Lola Jones

PLAY ALONG: *Discover The Vibration of Your Large Self*

Tuning in to the vibration of your Large Self gets easier as you increasingly open yourself to the relationship. Soon, you will easily be able to feel yourself into resonance with it simply by intention. It's always as close as The Presence. Some people, however, want something a bit more tangible to help them feel this vibration in the beginning. If you do, try this delicious meditation.

- Bring your awareness to the Earth, this miraculous breathing ball of life spinning through space, providing the literal stuff of your body and the ground for your being. Allow yourself to feel the incomprehensible miracle of it and your gratitude for the pure beauty and bounty it daily provides.
- Bring your focus to a specific place in nature that you love and honor its unique magnificence and the particular joy it has brought to you.
- When your love has grown large, send it into the Earth (intend and imagine this happening).
- Pause and let yourself receive the swell of love returning; it is always returned. Feel it in your body. Savor the vibration of Earth's rock-solid love for you.
- Then turn your awareness to the Sky and let yourself dissolve into its infinite expansion. Your mind may not like its complete inability to grasp this experience but the Larger, unlimited part of you will soar in recognition and awe. Settle there.
- When your love grows large, send it to the Sky.
- In the space of your pause, feel your love returned and savor the vibration of the Sky's boundless love for you.
- Deepen into this love between Earth, Sky and you. In this meeting, feel the vibrational essence of who and what you are: physical—dense, finite, limited; Non-Physical—expanded, infinite, unlimited; and the awareness of and appreciation for the dynamic, intrinsically creative interplay between them. This *is* your Divine nature. This is the vibration of God. The experience is one of completeness, and it can only be known when you bring it to life through you.

Note: Although I make up "steps" for certain experiences, it is solely for the comfort of the small self, who appreciates having specific things to do, especially in the beginning. In truth, reality is not linear: at any moment you can blast off and experience what you want directly. In reality, there's really just *one* step. You never need to do this or any particular step-by-step process to get where you want, but in the beginning they can help. They make certain states feel more accessible, and they help you navigate and explore new vibrational territories until eventually, you can get there easily, by intention.

❖

Creating With The Divine

The nature of The Divine is to create, and this is your nature too. When you align with The Presence within, life becomes less about fixing what's been and instead about creating anew. Your Large Self never looks back. It is firmly planted here with an eye towards what it can create to expand even more. When you are in your natural state, moving with the flow of Life, you are too.

"The Indweller knows your unspoken needs.
When you feel bad, The Indweller hears that you want to feel good,
and creates what you want.
All you have to do it step into it."
Lola Jones

Creation always happens as soon as you ask; the energetic matrix of what you want is created instantly in the Non-Physical. Your Large Self is already experiencing the vibration of what you want. Turning towards your Large Self is the most direct route there, and turning towards what you want is the most direct route to your Large Self! The game is rigged in your favor as long as you remember to keep yourself facing towards what feels good!!

⏸ *PAUSE AND REFLECT on The Unconditional Generosity Of God*
"The basic formula (to create) is: you ask (or feel a need,) The Indweller answers, you let it in." (Lola Jones, page 52.)

- The *ease* of creation can be hard for people to accept and let in. It's the second part *("The Indweller answers")* that we have a hard time believing, which makes the third part seem almost incomprehensible—and therefore difficult.
- You can't force yourself to accept the absolute and unconditional generosity of God, but you can intend to. When you really get that The Indweller *does* answer, no matter what, barriers to your creations begin to fall away.
- If you are ashamed of what you want, or believe your desires are wrong, bad, or not important enough for God to care about, or that you are not worthy to have what you want, you are putting the brakes on your creations, your awakening, and on your joy.
- Your Large Self is always facing the direction you say you want to go and enjoying it already. If you are facing away from it, focusing on the lack of it or your unworthiness to having it, you'll miss your Large Self jumping up and down and shouting, "Yes! It's perfect! It's already here—come on!" It doesn't matter what "it" is; it's all perfect to your Large Self!
- What future manifestation is your Large Self currently celebrating?!?

▶ *PLAY ALONG: Get Out Of The Way And Let It In*
"The Indweller always grants the essence of your request and just waits for the crack of an opening to fulfill it in the material world. Grace does 90%. Your only job, your 10%, is to get out of the way and let it in." (Lola Jones, page 52.)

- Getting out of the way takes awareness and practice.
- Some of the ways you may get in the way are: feeling unworthy; thinking you have to earn what you want; believing you have to fix what's wrong before you can feel right; thinking that life is about struggle and lessons; and not trusting that God cares about you and your needs.
- If there are things currently happening in your life that you don't want, are *you* inadvertently providing resistance? How could you let go and turn towards what you want—even a little?
- Stand up and do this now: feel the burden of old beliefs, unworthiness and resistance in your body and then physically turn your body in another direction. Turn towards ease, towards Grace doing 90%, towards new possibility, towards more joy.
- Repeat as necessary.

Bow to the Presence within.

Section Three Mantra: Take It To The Presence

GRACE IN ACTION

Dear Stranger,

Your comment brought me to my knees.

But while I was there, I bowed to The Presence within.

I held nothing back. I offered myself fully.

I shared my blazing rage, my white-hot shame, my blistering grief. I let the burn turn me inside out until each raw nerve had been exposed to the unconditioned generosity of cool, fresh air.

I was not alone. I met Myself there. And because of this holy communion, a lump of pain fell away and I was freed.

When I rose, things were different. I was different. I was more than I was.

And I knew, more than before, that in The Presence, through the eternal love and acceptance of The Presence, my burden is lessened, my heart is lifted, and my desires are answered.

Thank you Stranger.

*"The Presence within us hums along at its high, fine vibration
no matter what is going on in our mundane and very human lives.
Whether we humans awaken or not, and no matter how our lives go,
from its high vibration, the Essence Of Life enjoys living through us.
God never dips down into the lower vibrations as we do, no matter what happens.
God always sees infinite possibilities, offers solutions,
and holds the vibration of bliss for us as a steady homing signal."*
Lola Jones

Section Four: Go With The Flow

Nurturing Your Relationship With The Divine

Your Large Self is magnetic. Its attraction is constant, expressed as anything that inspires or helps you to feel better and more alive, expansive and connected, moment by moment.

Your small self is also magnetic. When your overall vibration is low (when you are closer to the bottom of the Instrument Panel), small self exerts its own force, keeping you focused on problems, bad news, scary stories, and things that don't feel good—convincing you that you can't move forward until you fix what's wrong. It's just what small self does, but it's easy to get hypnotized by the pull of its wrong-seeking, backwards-facing focus. From this orbit, it's hard to feel the forward-facing gravitational attraction of Large Self.

Fortunately, Grace can help to override the hypnotic influence of small-self! It gives you a vibrational boost, lifting and pointing you in a better feeling direction. Then it's up to you to keep yourself pointed in that direction. To do so, you must be willing to make new choices.

The conscious-mind training in Divine Openings shows you how to choose differently. You learn to acknowledge emotional energy and allow it to move, which feels better than avoiding and resisting. You start to recognize scary stories and begin telling ones that feel better. You learn to focus on what you want, not what you don't. You remember that you can always let go and ask The Divine for help.

Your vibration rises, and as it does, you are increasingly drawn into the orbit of Large Self. Up there, all is well. The Flow of Life is trusted. You create with ease and Grace. Things start making sense again.

You lived in this high vibrational state until the lower vibrations of those around you pulled you into their orbit. Your natural vibration of *joy* and *positive expectation* was trained out of you by well-meaning adults, and as you joined them in focusing more on what didn't feel good, you lost touch with your own inner guidance to focus on what does. As a result, the world may have begun to feel unsafe.

By Grace (90%) and by heeding the ever-present invitation of your Large Self to reorient towards what's good, true and real (your 10%), you come back into innocence, connection and trust. Life on Earth makes sense once again, even with all its contrasting experiences.

When you nurture the relationship with your Large Self and make it *the* primary relationship in your life, you plug into the true Source of your power. When this power is flowing in your life, living becomes an exciting, ever-unfolding, adventure.

⏸ PAUSE AND REFLECT on Your Direct Experience With The Divine

The relationship you have with your Large Self reflects *your* expectations and openness.

- Do you still believe you need an intermediary to experience The Divine within?
- If you still depend on rituals, intermediaries and props to help connect, the relationship will reflect this distance. Go within and keep your connection simple, uncomplicated and direct.

**Your Large Self is everywhere you are.
Are you tuning in?**

- When you speak with your Large Self, it is casual or do you put distance between you, as if speaking to someone in authority? Do you expect to be shamed, judged and made wrong? Do you brace for bad news? Do you feel safe enough to relax and receive?
- Begin to notice your interactions with people of authority—people you perceive as having more power than you or power over you. Does your body tighten up? Do you find it easy to hear and let in what they are saying?
- What happens to your sense of self? Do you contract into yourself? Do you expand into their space? Are you able to simply meet them, energetically?
- Notice and explore this experience. Don't judge; bring awareness and curiosity instead.
- Remember, Divine Openings doesn't ask you to fix anything. If you notice distance between you and your Large Self, this awareness can inspire a new desire for connection. As you increasingly focus on the relationship you want to have, you move in that direction. Grace supercharges your focus, intention and willingness!

◐ PLAY ALONG: Prostrate, Surrender And Let The Divine Do The Heavy Lifting

Prostrating is the only specific practice that Lola brought home from her twenty-one days in India. When you prostrate, you literally lay down your concerns and surrender them to The Divine. Prostrating demonstrates your trust while also deepening it.

- Is there something too big for you to figure out right now? Something that you just want help with or relief from?
- Lay your body on the floor and consciously allow yourself to let it all go. Surrender completely. Trust it to the infinite resources of your Large Self.
- Can you feel that when you let go completely, you are still held? By *something*?
- Relax into the knowing that your needs and desires are heard; deepen and rest in this sublime, confident allowing.
- When you feel complete, turn your attention elsewhere and *let* The Divine do the heavy lifting. Go have fun!
- Really do this and keep doing it as needed: we tend to habitually pick back up the things we've laid down. Make a new habit!

◐ PLAY ALONG: Tune In, Often

Your Large Self always wants to hear from you, not just when you need help. Everything can be lightened by the love Large Self feels for you. This is a gift you can give to yourself at any moment.

- Right now, what good news will you celebrate with The Presence within? What can you share about your hopes and dreams? About what excites and sparks your passion and aliveness?
- The Presence knows already but it adores hearing from you so it can lovingly reflect back, "Yes, I know."
- Describe, dance, or draw how "Yes, I know" feels in your body!

*"Resisting unwanted aspects of yourself only strengthens them.
What you resist persists.
Just watch them come and go, observe them as energies, and embrace them all.
Awareness is all you need to over time become more your authentic core self."*
Lola Jones

Letting Go To The Flow

Resistance to Life is always the cause of suffering. We live in a world of contrast, and unwanted experiences and feelings will arise, no matter how enlightened we become. But pushing against them is counter to Life's current, which always wants to move us forward, towards realization of the fresh desires that are inspired by contrast! When Life feels bad, it's nudging us awake, to make choices that let that energy move. Our resistance to feeling momentary bad feelings keeps them from moving towards better.

Letting go of resistance happens in every moment you choose not to run. Whatever is right now—simply because it is happening is enough of a reason to find a way to face and accept it. Even if you don't like what's happening, your response is much more effective from a place of acceptance than from resistance. Acceptance can be as simple as, "Okay, this is happening. Now what?"

As you stop actively *pushing against*, you begin to automatically reorient with the Flow of Life, which is always moving forward, in the direction of *Yes*. The comfort you have been seeking is discovered when you become willing to engage with yourself, and Life, in The Presence. The deeper your relationship with The Presence becomes, the easier it is to let go and go with the flow—to let go and let The Divine do the heavy lifting and move your forward, towards feelings and experiences you want. Softening is the essence of this relationship. As you soften and relax, you begin to experience the profound trustworthiness of Life, and you simply begin to feel better.

⏸ *PAUSE AND REFLECT on Making Space For Fresh Desire To Flow*

When you are swimming against the tide, life can be about drama and struggle. Seeking and chronic busyness result from habitually trying to avoid, fix or change what feels bad.

If you have identified with drama or being a seeker, when you finally get turned in the right direction you may feel a sense of loss. Instead of rushing to fill the space drama once filled, occupy it. If you are aware of uncomfortable feelings or the urge to rush into the next doing, pause. Intend to give the feelings space so they can move. When they do—from that higher vibration—better feeling, drama-free desires will arise. Increasingly, as you move up the Instrument Panel, actions will result from *excitement* and *positive expectation*, not from *fear* and *lack*, and the life you create will be filled with adventure, not drama.

- What are some ways you habitually fill empty time and space in your life?
- Do you give yourself time to really look, listen and hear? To feel?
- Do you give space to what is, so fresh, better feeling desire can build?
- Right now, how can you give yourself the gifts of time and space?

⏸ *PAUSE AND REFLECT on Appreciating The Flow Of Grace*

Life is meant to flow and Life is good. And this flow of goodness sustains and surrounds you and streams down constantly even when you are resisting and choosing not to let it in. There are bound to be moments when these sweet, Grace-filled waters seep through your sometimes-parched armor.

*"When you regain the innocence of a child,
there is nothing too silly to do if it will get a laugh,
so be generous with your laughter.
I remember reading somewhere that polite European society used to deem it
unrefined to laugh out loud, and so they suppressed their laughter,
allowing only a slight smirk to betray their amusement,
lest they look like commoners.
There are remnants of that old belief hanging around today,
and I am so glad to be free to laugh and show my appreciation and delight."*
Lola Jones

- When they do, will you lay down your struggle, at least for that moment?
- Will you acknowledge the moments of peace, when they come? Will you honor them, celebrate them, *embody* them?
- Life is not meant to be a battle. Your appreciation is a momentary truce. Surrender, often.

▶ PLAY ALONG: Learn The Vibration Of Appreciation

Appreciation puts you in the flow. It is a powerful vibration to know. Once you recognize and learn this or *any* vibration, you can easily generate it.

- Focus on something or someone you truly, deeply appreciate. Surrender and settle into the sensations appreciation generates in body. Give your most exquisite attention to how it feels.
- Allow the waves of appreciation to swell. Let them break apart any crust around your heart.
- Find the pulse of appreciation there, in your heart. Feel it, memorize it, and learn how to feel your way back there at any time. Create a new preset on your emotional dial.

▶ PLAY ALONG: Use Humor To Lighten Up Your Life!

Humor is a powerful way to relax, let go and enjoy the ride. It helps you lighten up and feel better, which are both characteristics of the enlightened experience.

- How could you bring more humor, fun and joy into your life? As you do, you relax, and more Grace is able to flow.
- Lola's expression "coughing up a hairball" injects a little ease and humor into situations that might feel, in the moment, difficult and serious. The truth is, sometimes big energy needs to move and it doesn't feel good! Lightening up about it helps you feel better now and lets the energy move faster.
- If there is currently some super-heavy "issue" or situation weighing you down, can you find any way lighten up about it? Certainly there are times when life is serious, but these are times it's especially important to find ways to feel better—if even for brief moments. Always, the lighter our touch, the easier it is for things to move.
- What will you do this week to encourage more ease and laughter? How can you bring more fun into your household? Are you willing to do things completely out of character, be silly and look for ways to laugh and have fun?
- Bring lightness into your world and watch as the people around you begin to lighten up too!

▶ PLAY ALONG: Use Awareness To Lighten Up Your Body!

Enlightenment is physical. Paradoxically, when you really slow down, show up and drop into your experience, you allow things to move and rise, and everything lightens up! Your body becomes less dense and more alive as the higher energies take root, and this feels exhilarating!

There is a constant stream of energy flowing through your body. *Feel it.*

You can accelerate this process by choosing to bring more awareness into your body now. Awareness softens, relaxes and helps things move. It bathes your cells in love, and everything is lifted by love.

- Start with your hand, or your foot, and intend to *feel it from the inside*.
- Don't focus your awareness *on* it, like a laser; that's a mental activity—seeing it from the outside.
- Instead, ease awareness *into*; sense your hand, or foot, from the inside.
- Let your awareness be a soft, warm light and allow it to gently fill your body with its soothing glow.
- Attend to your physical experience.
- There is a constant stream of energy flowing through your body. Feel it!

When we ignore the choice that feels better, we resist the pull of The Divine.

Section Four Mantra: Go With The Flow

GRACE IN ACTION

Resistance is painful. More than what we are resisting, it is our resistance to it that causes the most pain. We think our resistance will protect us, but in the end it only turns against us, turning us upstream, against the natural Flow of Life. Essentially, it turns us against ourselves.

What do we resist? We resist things that don't feel good, or things that we're afraid won't feel good, or things that didn't feel good in the past. Often we resist because it's just become a habit. Our default has become *No*.

When we judge ourselves for not being who or what or how or where we believe we "should" be, and when we judge others for being exactly who and what and how and where they are now, we are in resistance to Life, which never judges.

When we reject or deny what is happening because we're afraid we won't be able to handle it, we resist allowing our true power to emerge.

When we avoid feeling something because we're afraid we'll get stuck in it, or be swallowed up by it, we resist experiencing that things do flow and rise, when we let them.

When we ignore the choice that feels better, we resist the call of The Divine.

When we resist dropping into The Presence, we resist communing with and experiencing our True Nature.

And when we build barriers to the giving and receiving of love (especially to ourselves), we resist the most powerful force in this universe.

Feel how much work all this takes. Are you ready to not work quite so hard?

Life *is*. Things happen that don't feel good *and* that cause you to want to feel even better. This is the nature of contrast and it's an integral, necessary part of life. Contrast shows where energy wants to move and where you are ready to expand. It invites you to get curious about what story you may be telling or what beliefs and expectations are being acted out. It reminds you to let go and ask for help—to remember that you are never alone and powerless. Contrast always clarifies and brings forth desire—if you let it.

Contrast is a tune your Large Self hums to get your attention. Contrast can sing your expansion into existence, but it needs you to get in harmony with it. When you judge, reject, avoid, ignore, resist and build barriers to its invitation, you stop the music.

As you start to appreciate the role of contrast in your life, you become less afraid of things that don't feel good, and the hold of fear and resistance begins to soften. Cracks develop in your habits; Grace can now enter and soften you even more.

Breathe in and breathe out, contract and let go, and notice how each part allows for more. This is the rhythm of Life, constantly pulsing. This is the rhythm of you, forever expanding.

Cherish each part of this eternal dance; they're both part of the same sacred flow.

Section Five: Choose Your Focus

Every Desire Is A Call From Home

No matter what specific desires may have led you to the spiritual path (happier relationship, better health, more money), they are all echoes of a larger desire to experience the true fulfillment your Large Self feels. Every desire, large or small, is a call from Home. Implicit in every want and need is the desire to feel better, and feeling better is what expands you into alignment with your Large Self.

Your desires are Divinely inspired! They expand you and all of Creation. Recognizing and attending to their Source is a shortcut to their fulfillment. Finding ways to soothe yourself and feel better now about what you want is another. These are things the small self needs practice doing.

The small self lives in a state of inner scarcity and insecurity. Cut off from the unlimited abundance of the Large Self, its desires are fueled by *fear, craving, jealousy* and other vibrations of lack: in order to feel good, it has to *do* this or *have* that. Unfortunately, when you place limits and conditions on our happiness, your happiness is limited and conditional! Desires that spring from lack cannot lead to true fulfillment.

In Divine Openings you are invited and shown how to be independently happy and fulfilled. You learn to provide soothing and safety to yourself—or find it in your relationship with your Large Self—independent of outer events. You reclaim power to feel *accepting, optimistic* and even *appreciative* no matter what shows up in the external world. As a result, the sense of inner lack dissipates, replaced by the generous knowledge of your own inner power and plenty. Since desires emerge from greater *security* and *contentment*, this is what starts being reflected back in your outer experience.

Wanting, dreaming and expanding are essential parts of life in a physical body. They are supposed to feel good! And they do when you are already fulfilled. So when desires arise, widen your lens: attend to the Source of their call. Bring your focus within and nurture your relationship with The Presence.

In this relationship, lack is replaced by security, so money can flow more easily. Old tensions, worries and stress fall away, allowing health to improve. When you experience inner harmony, you attract outer relationships that reflect this fulfillment.

⏸ *PAUSE AND REFLECT on the Importance Of Feeling Good*

Our culture has diminished the importance of feeling good. We weren't meant to suffer, but suffering is glorified as ordinary and even honorable, and we've become trapped by its narrative.

- If you want to feel better, you must change the narrative—and your focus. Everything that lifts your spirit, gives you hope, eases your burden, offers relief, and inspires happiness and joy contains a message from The Divine: turn *this* way, make *that* choice to feel better.
- Are your ears open to these messages? They are everywhere, all the time, even in things that don't necessarily feel good—sometimes especially in things that don't feel good! "Turn around," they are saying: "Don't get stuck here! Bounce towards what feels better!"

"Try this: tense up and clench your muscles, your jaw, your shoulders, ball up your fists.
Imagine someone trying to give you something to make you feel better when you're like that.
That's what resistance is.
Now relax and hold out your open hands.
Now you can receive.
It's humanity's Ancient Mind conditioning that keeps us tense and resistant.
We can't fix it ourselves, but Grace can, without effort.
Just say yes. Say it out loud right now. YES! Keep saying yes."

Lola Jones

- Kids bounce naturally. But as they get pulled into the vibrational gravity of those around them, they become more like Velcro and begin sticking to unwanted things.
- Fortunately, Grace is the antidote to anything sticky. Grace is restoring your bounciness, but *you* still have to be willing, moment by moment, to actually bounce!
- Every moment offers a choice, and the choice that feels better offers new, expanded possibilities. What possibility could this moment hold? Choose that. Bounce towards that!

▶ PLAY ALONG: Feel the YES In Your Desire

Feeling better about the things you want reduces your resistance to letting them in.

- Pause. Acknowledge something you want right now. Allow the desire to seep into your cells so you can feel the wanting in your body.
- Ask: "How am I feeling about this desire?" and locate it on the Instrument Panel. The possibilities range from *numb*, *apathetic*, and *unworthy* to *relaxed*, *hopeful* and even *ecstatic!*
- If you have trouble pinpointing how you feel (or even if you don't), ask: "How does this desire feel *in my body?* Where am I feeling it?" Check in with your body.
- Is your body relaxed and open—ready, willing and able to let it in? Or is your body clenched or tight—readying, perhaps, to fight for it? Can you imagine and celebrate the presence of what you want or are focusing on the absence of it?
- Now imagine that your Divine Presence knows and is thrilled by what you want! Really do this! Imagine the Non-Physical excitement that is gathering around this desire. Imagine your Large Self saying, "This and more is already here where I am!" Can you feel the invitation from your Large Self to turn and join it in its revelry of joyous expansion?
- How do you feel now? Has it shifted? Can you find this new feeling on the Instrument Panel?
- What if you could celebrate the invitation, implicit in *every* desire, to feel better right now?

▶ PLAY ALONG: Focus Again (Always!) On States Of Being

The fastest and easiest path to the things you want is to focus on the state of being you desire.

- You did this in Section One, but you'll deepen it here. Choose one thing that you desire to *do* or *have* and consider the state of *being* that best reflects what the having or doing will give you.
- Perhaps you want to lose weight (doing). The states of being you may want are to feel *healthy, happy, strong* or *confident*. Or perhaps you want a better car (having). The states of being you might want are to feel *secure, powerful, reliable*, or even more *sexy* and *alive!*
- Not all of these states are listed on the Instrument Panel. Nevertheless, you can plot any feeling or state of being on the Instrument Panel—where it feels most appropriate *to you*. This is a good habit to cultivate.
- Plot where you are now, relative to your desire, and then identify and plot where you'd like to be when your desire is fulfilled. This is your map. In the next sections you'll practice deliberately using this map to get from here to there.

*"Even though Divine Grace is lifting you up,
you either use your Free Will to go with Grace or to resist it.
Your attention is powerful.
When you consistently focus upon what you want,
it's like pointing the nose of your plane toward it.
You end up where your nose is pointed.
Focus on where you want to go and you arrive there, in time..."*
Lola Jones

- In the meantime, know that any desired state of being is most easily fulfilled in your relationship with The Divine. Your Large Self already experiences itself—already experiences *you*—the way you wish to experience yourself: healthy, strong, attractive, confident, secure, powerful, even sexy! When you are aligned with your Large Self, you experience these states too and simply magnetize the things you thought you needed to achieve those states.
- Ask The Divine to show you how it sees you. Intend to *feel* the answer. Then let go and take action as guided. Let The Divine take care of the details.
- Remember, what is important to you is important to The Presence, and to Life. Trust that fresh motivation, new inspiration and unlimited possibilities are eternally unfolding and endlessly available. The path to what you want is much, much wider than you think.

❖

Practicing A New, Forward-Focus
Your power of focus and attention is a great ability and gift, and because you are waking up, this gift is becoming increasingly available to you. When you slow down and show up, you have choices: you can focus on what you don't want or are lacking, or you can focus your attention in the direction of *Yes*. Which feels better? From which direction can you hear the call of your Large Self?

Much of mankind remains under the spell of Ancient Mind and the small-self mindset that focuses primarily on problems: change happens from fixing what's "wrong" *out there*, usually with great effort.

Divine Openings unhooks you from Ancient mind and plugs you into pure Source energy. It becomes easier to vibrate more in harmony with your Large Self, turn from what you don't want, and simply create anew.

But even though you're becoming increasingly free from the grip of a wrong-seeking, problem-oriented, backwards-focused mind, it's still up to you to continually choose a new direction, until it becomes habit. Old habits are powerful. Choosing anew takes practice.

 PAUSE AND REFLECT on Telling A Better Story
"Telling a better story" is one choice that becomes increasingly accessible with Divine Openings. Telling a better story nudges your vibration in a better feeling direction. You can tell a better story about something happening in the moment or after the fact; the point is to begin to notice when the mind is spinning scary stories and then being able to comfort and soothe it with the new language (and vibration) you are learning. This is something you'll practice to again and again.

- Consider a recent experience that did not happen the way you hoped. How could you begin to shift from *discouragement* or *disappointment* or *frustration* towards *acceptance*?
- "I don't need to like it. I just need to be willing to accept that it is, indeed, happening."
- "When I accept what's happening, at least I'm not making it worse by resisting or denying it."
- "I wonder what my Large Self feels about this."
- "Everything is temporary; this too shall pass—if I let it!"

*"Until appreciation becomes a minute-by-minute habit for you,
a morning and evening time of 'raving and appreciating'
lifts your altitude and your attitude until you naturally reach equanimity,
then you are free of the mind and its judgments."*
Lola Jones

- Could you reach for *appreciation*?
- "At the very least, it's an opportunity to reclaim power by feeling my feelings about it."
- "Now I know what I don't want, and my clarity about what I do want is stronger than ever."
- "I wonder what new, exciting desires and possibilities are unfolding from this experience!"

⏸ PAUSE AND REFLECT on *Choosing Acceptance*

Accepting something that's happening (in the world or in yourself) is one of the most powerful choices you can make. Accepting does not necessarily mean condoning or even liking what you're feeling or what has happened. It simply means you are no longer resisting it. Acceptance is more than halfway up the Instrument Panel. From lower vibrations, it might not always be easy to choose acceptance, but you can intend to soften towards it.

- Acceptance unfolds from *Yes*. You can't necessarily push yourself into it; you relax into *Yes* as you stop judging, making wrong, avoiding, denying and pushing away.
- Can you feel the vibration of *Yes* in your body? Express how it feels; do it in color!!
- Acceptance is where magic really begins to happen. Acceptance is like a launching pad. From *Yes*, you can blast off quickly towards anywhere!
- Right now, where could you soften into acceptance?

▶ PLAY ALONG: *Appreciate And Rave!!*

Appreciation is another choice that becomes easier with Divine Openings. Appreciation has a high vibration and gets you pointed towards your Large Self. When you can find things to appreciate about any situation, your enlightenment is truly beginning to flower. When you consistently, eagerly *look for* things to appreciate, you know your Large Self is in the driver's seat.

Raving is active, focused appreciation. Raving is one of the most powerful things you can to do steadily train your attention and raise your vibration. Raving is magic.

- Right now, can you rave out loud for five minutes? Look around: Look for beauty and abundance and declare your appreciation!
- Is there color your eyes can enjoy? Are birds gifting your ears with song? Is there food in the cabinets? Do you have water and electricity? A place to sleep? Is there someone you love? Is the sun shining (or the rain falling)? Is your heart beating and are you alive on this day that is filled with new possibility and potential?
- If you can't rave for five minutes, intend to work up to it! Your voice has a potent vibration, especially when expressing love and appreciation. Raving out loud enhances its power!
- There is a Facebook group called The Daily Rave that was started by Divine Openings Guide Marleen Renders. Outside of the Divine Openings website it is one of the most high-vibe, feel-good places you can find on the Internet. Even if you don't post, take time to stop by and give yourself the gift of this powerful attitude adjustment.

"When we judge, loath or criticize ourselves and resist aspects of ourselves instead of just experiencing them and allowing them to be, there is war within us. When we are disconnected from our Large Self that is always peaceful, there is war within. When there is struggle and unrest within our own families, it is the same energy as war."

Lola Jones

Focusing On Peace In Relationships

Although Grace is helping you unhook from Ancient Mind, recognize that not everyone is having this experience. There is a lot of suffering and conflict in the world.

A world at war reflects people at war within themselves; people hooked into the energy of war simply cannot authentically relate with others. Shaming, judging or pushing against their armor only reinforces the underlying consciousness that created it—when pushed, people usually push back. Most everyone you meet is fighting their own battle. Don't add to it. Patience, acceptance and understanding are important. You can't share them with others until you've given them to yourself.

How you relate to others reflects your current consciousness like nothing else. Peace in outer relationships indicates that you have allowed peace to take hold inside. When you are no longer afraid to meet yourself in whatever feeling or experience you are having, you can truly meet others in peace.

Enlightened relationships are defined by this high level of self- and other-acceptance. Grace naturally orients you in this direction, towards this Large-Self experience, but you must accept the invitation, moment by moment, to soften towards the parts of yourself you judge and condemn. When you do, peace and acceptance ripple into the world.

The most powerful stance you can occupy in any relationship is solid, certain, accepting and inviting; you allow your vibration to declare: "Come join me!" You don't push or pull—you attract. You allow the other to be as they are while vibrationally inviting them to soften, expand and join you in peace.

ⅠⅠ *PAUSE AND REFLECT on Bringing Peace To Your Relationships*

If you are holding on to old wounds and if you have closed your heart to key people in your life, *you* are suffering and your other relationships will reflect this. Love, like Life and Grace, wants to flow. Letting it is essential if you want to experience the freedom and peace you have likely been seeking.

To clean up your relationships, you do not need to know *how*. Willingness and a desire to be free are all you need. If you are sincere, the Presence within will either shift them for you or provide the means. Life provides countless opportunities *now* to let energy move and shift. Your job is to be awake and not resist the opportunities.

- So the question becomes, do you truly want to be free, and will you let it be easy? Are there still barriers to believing it can be easy?
- Grace will do the heavy lifting in your relationships, but you must be willing to do your part. Do the activity at the end of this section in *Things Are Going Great In My Absence* (page 82).
- Really do it! Don't forfeit the opportunity to reclaim power. Allow fresh energy and intention to move through all your relationships! This will transform your life, and your world.
- If there are still relationships where you are withholding love or that you are "working on," focus instead on your relationship with The Presence. Every relationship reflects that one.
- Have you taken time today to tend to that relationship? How can you open to it even more?

Seeing and accepting others as they are is powerful love.
To share it, you must be willing to give it to yourself, first.

⏸ *PAUSE AND REFLECT on Your Beliefs About Judgment and Forgiveness*

"It feels more accurate to me to say, 'I've stopped judging you,' than to say, 'I forgive you.'" (Lola Jones, page 79.)

- Is there someone you have been unable to forgive? Do you think your Large Self has forgiven them? Did your Large Self ever judged them in the first place?
- Your answer is meaningful; it reveals what you may believe about your own intrinsic guilt or innocence. Do you believe *you* are judged? Do you believe *you* require forgiveness?
- Your Large Self doesn't judge because it doesn't see the world through the lens of duality—as good and bad or wrong and right. There's never anything for it to forgive.
- How might it feel for you to see things from this perspective? What would you need to let go of? Are you willing to experiment with seeing things from a Large-Self perspective?
- Let your small self play with the questions. There are no wrong answers.

▶ *PLAY ALONG: See The World From Large-Self Perspective*

Your Large Self doesn't judge. It accepts everyone, including you. The more you practice seeing from this perspective the more all your relationships will flourish. It is a magnificent gift to the world.

- Take a moment today and intend to step into a larger perspective. Close your eyes, form the slightest smile on your lips, and soften your breath, your body, and your awareness. Allow your attention to widen and become more spacious and diffuse. Attend to the expansiveness within and without.
- Then, from this open and allowing perspective, gaze into the eyes of a lover, a child, a pet or even yourself, through a mirror. Take them in gently, exactly as they are. Intend, from your expansion, to see the expansiveness in them. *See them*. You'll feel it when you do.
- So will they. Notice how they respond. Give them the space to simply respond as they do.
- When you give others this space to simply *be*, you become even bigger than you were.
- Intend to really see the people in your life, as best as you are able. Let people know that you see them. Recognize the gift in this and offer it freely.

▶ *PLAY ALONG: Focus On The Gifts of Grace*

You are now halfway through *Things Are Going Great In My Absence*. You have been learning how to use your Free Will to maximum benefit and retraining your mind to stay out of the way so Grace can flow more freely. And Grace *is* flowing! Pause now and reflect on what has changed.

- Look at the Instrument Panel and acknowledge where you were when you started (you did this on page 13).
- Where are you now? How has The Divine already done some of the heavy lifting? What has changed "in your absence?" Where, and when, is there greater flow?
- Take time to really acknowledge and appreciate what has changed—and how easily it has.
- What you focus on expands, so write about your experience here before moving on.

If you're not choosing, what is?

Section Five Mantra: Choose Your Focus

GRACE IN ACTION
Several months ago as I begrudgingly schlepped through an unplanned late-afternoon shopping trip, Grace slipped through a crack and shook me loose from the trance I was in. I happened to look up and my awareness was met by the multi-colored walls marking the different grocery sections. I had never noticed them. Their cheery hue contrasted my mood and gave me pause...

...which, gratefully, I was willing to accept. I stopped. I looked. I really looked.

Immediately, my brittle, inward-focused and tightly-wrapped energy rose up and billowed out. Everything shifted. I could suddenly breathe and see: I was in the market! Other people were around! I was delivered back into the world, reconnected, whole and awake.

Without the contrast of my prior mood, this opening might not have been so sweet. And though Grace perhaps nudged me awake on this occasion, I learned a lot about how I can arrive there more purposefully.

The painted walls in that particular store have become a deliberate reminder to wake up and pay attention. They also remind me, week after week, that *anything* can be such a touchstone. A beloved tree, a stranger's eyes, the sound of a car horn, and especially the sensations in my own body can pull me back into the soft *Yes* of this moment, if I allow them to.

At any moment you can wake up, and every awakened moment carries the possibility of a new choice: what will you focus on now?

If you're not choosing, what is?

"We're evolving away from the judgment and the suffering caused by the mind's domination.
We don't have to know how to do it.
Our desire births solutions in the vast Unlimited Intelligence,
and we take steps as guided."
Lola Jones

Section Six: Just Say Yes

Your Nature Is To Expand

You are gaining momentum, moving energy, embodying your Divinity, and learning to create at a very high, conscious level. You are being shown how to manage Free Will choices to deliberately maximize this momentum, and the Grace from Divine Openings is helping you sustain increasingly higher vibrations. As energy is moving, your desires are continually being clarified, and as long as you're not contradicting, judging or otherwise limiting them, you are expanding in their direction.

You haven't had to fight to make this happen. You haven't had to earn your expansion or prove yourself worthy of it or make it happen through hard work and struggle. You've simply needed show up, play with new practices and ideas, act when guided, and allow it. This is your 10%.

Your 10% is mostly about tuning in and moving closer, vibrationally, to the part of you that already knows your worth and recognizes your expanded nature. You still act, but as you close the vibrational gap between you and your Large Self, you are increasingly pulled into its powerful, knowing orbit, and clearer guidance and easier, more inspired action naturally result from this movement.

You close the gap by accepting *this* experience and *this* feeling, moment by moment, choice by choice. It is the loveliest paradox: your acceptance of *this* allows you to expand into *more* than this! You don't expand because there is anything wrong with you or this moment; nothing is wrong—even if you don't like what's happening. Instead, you expand because you are part of Creation and the nature of Creation is to want more and create more, endlessly. Life is always expanding, and this is your nature too. You are always moving morewards!

Divine Openings helps you reconcile the paradox that this moment is perfect and whole and acceptable—*and* you want more. You don't reconcile it with your mind; this isn't something you can understand. You reconcile it naturally and with increasing frequency when you experience a wide-open *Yes* while also feeling the giddy *excitement* and *joy* of "More Please"—all in the same heartbeat.

⏸ PAUSE AND REFLECT on Claiming Your Worthiness To Be And Have More

True worthiness isn't arrogant, but neither is it falsely humble or self-deprecating. You cannot claim it if you judge being worthy as egotistic, selfish or naughty! Your Large Self knows your intrinsic worth and celebrates your every desire to be and have what you want. Decide to agree with it!

- Are there people you judge for embracing their true, authentic, fabulous selves, living as if they had nothing to apologize for and wanting and accepting all the gifts that Life bestows?
- Are there ways you judge or hold back from celebrating yourself? Do you ever feel compelled to apologize for your existence? For wanting what you want? For wanting more?
- Try this on for size: "I am magnificent as I am, and worthy of all of Life's blessings."
- What happens in your body when you say this? How near, or far, from *Yes* do you feel? It's good to know where you are. Just notice. Awareness makes space for *Yes* to emerge.

This moment is all there is.
Your body is an anchor to this moment.
Use it to come back, again and again and again.

▶ PLAY ALONG: *Let Yourself Be Loved and Expanded*

You'll receive specific processes to more deliberately move energy and raise your worthiness vibration in the next sections, but for now—and this can't be repeated enough!—the best way to loosen the grip of unworthiness is spending time in The Presence and communing with the Larger part of you that already knows your worth. Each time you dip into the reality beyond mind and its story, the grip of unworthiness begins to loosen. Your Large Self broadcasts love and acceptance—even adoration—for who you are and where you are, right now. As your vibration rises, it becomes easier to hear. And, one of the fastest ways to raise your vibration is to commune with The Presence.

- What have you done today to nourish your inner connection? How can you invite more Presence into your life? In which daily activity could you consciously include your Large Self?
- Right now, decide to experience this connection. Close your eyes, drop into your body, and be with whatever is present. Breathe.
- Soften your focus and soften your heart. Allow yourself to feel the love and support that is always present for you.
- If this is hard to feel, then stand up and feel the ground beneath you. Really do this!
- Feel your feet on the floor and imagine the Earth below. Feel the support. Take a few steps and feel how you are supported when you are moving as well as when you are standing still—or even when taking a few steps backwards!
- Give the ground all of your weight. Notice how you are still supported. You don't have to work to make this happen, you don't have to earn it. It's the nature of ground to support you.
- It's the nature of The Divine to support you as well. You are always loved and dearly held, even if you don't feel worthy of it. It seems almost wasteful not to let it in and embrace it!

▶ PLAY ALONG: *Turning In The Right Direction*

Faster-moving emotional energy feels better than slower-moving energy. Nevertheless, some people get turned around and confuse slower, lower, "bad" feelings with feeling good: unworthiness, guilt and constant penance are valued by many in our world. Others have come to believe that it's safer to guard against disappointment and other lower feelings by not asking for much, so they hold themselves back by minimizing and denying their needs and desires. But holding back feels bad, and feeling bad can never lead to authentic feelings of safety. Neither can shame, suffering and other forms of self-punishment even lead to authentic feelings of worthiness and joy.

- To adjust an upside-down Instrument Panel, you need to learn how feelings feel *in your body*.
- Think of something you currently want and tune into how your body feels about it. You did this earlier, but now you'll go deeper.
- Your body communicates via sensation and you may not be familiar with its language, so give it time to speak. Pause, soften and allow the body to speak to you.
- Your mind may want to tell stories about what you want. This isn't story time. If thoughts arise, instead of pushing them away simply refocus your attention on any physical sensations you notice in your body. Get curious about them! Give your mind something else to do!

"Peace begins within each of us, with compassion and acceptance for ourselves —from a quiet, calm mind, allowing of all our parts and aspects. As all our scattered parts are accepted, valued, and experienced, they are soothed—they make peace."
Lola Jones

- If your desire is coming from a sense of lack, from *fear*, or from somewhere else low on the Instrument Panel, you generally will feel an inner constriction. Maybe your stomach will feel a bit clamped, or you breath will be tight, or there'll be a slight tension in your shoulders.
- Perhaps there will also be an overall emotional atmosphere of contraction.
- In the body's language, this usually indicates *No,* or *Not Yet*. It shows that your vibration about what you want is not aligned with what you say you want; you are facing away from it. Perhaps a part of you just does not believe you deserve the house, the relationship, the raise...
- If your desire is coming from higher on the Instrument Panel, from *acceptance,* perhaps, or even *positive expectation*, you may feel a *whoosh* of expansion, an inner loosening, or *excitement*. In the body's language, this is *Yes:* your vibration is more aligned with where you want to go; you are facing towards what you want. Getting there from this vibration is much easier!
- Being able to decipher the general physical and atmospheric feelings of *Yes* and *No* is helpful as you begin to tune into your inner Instrument Panel. *Yes* or *No* is essential feedback.
- Remember that the messages themselves—the *Yes* or the *No*—are neither good nor bad. They are solely indicators of how your desire feels to you at this moment. If the desire feels bad, that's good information to have! When you realize you're headed away where you want to go, there are things you can do to turn around.
- Letting yourself *feel* the physical contraction, or the *No,* is always a good place to start, and you do that more easily by not making it wrong. Feeling gets the energy moving, and when energy moves, you feel better! When you feel better, you're turning towards what you want.

▶ PLAY ALONG: *Expand How You See Yourself*

Are you someone who needs the acceptance of others to feel okay about yourself? That's like looking for your own image in someone else's reflection. It's a risky, harmful habit, and it doesn't work. Start with intending acceptance for yourself. Give to yourself what you want from others, or discover it in the relationship with your Large Self.

- Spend two minutes in front of a mirror for 30 days in a row with the willingness to accept and even rejoice in what you see and who you are! If it's hard, that's okay; it gets easier.
- Gaze softly with the intention to accept, celebrate and soothe. Let your magnificence arise!
- Put a sticky note on your bathroom mirror to remember to do this. You will be glad you did!

Creating Enlightened Connections

An accepting, generous, self-affirming relationship with The Presence gives you the foundation necessary for creating other enlightened relationships. When inner judgment, feelings of scarcity, and self-denial give way to a knowing of your own wholeness, outer relationships no longer have to fill unmet needs. From fulfillment, you attract relationships that are fulfilling. From self-acceptance, you can more easily accept others as they are. From increasing joy and happiness, you no longer make others responsible for your happiness and well-being, which makes you more attractive to them!

*"Appreciation is the same vibrational frequency as love.
Most humans have some highly charged and distorted concepts about love,
and may even find 'love' hard to muster when they're not happy with someone.
But the concept of appreciation is clear and clean,
so it's easier and simpler to call up appreciation than love.
Even if you can't conjure love for a person right now,
you can always authentically find something to appreciate about them."*
Lola Jones

When you let other people off the hook for your happiness and wellbeing, relationships really blossom. Unconditional love flows when you are happy no matter what the other person does.

⏸ PAUSE AND REFLECT on *Making Past Relationships Right*

Sometimes a relationship runs its course. Learning to let go without closing your heart keeps you oriented with the stream of Life. With Divine Openings, it becomes easier to appreciate what was, and move on. Your Large Self harbors no grudge, holds no anger, and sees no reason to forgive because it never judges or sees itself as a victim. Grace is moving you towards that experience.

- Are all your old relationships feeling free and clear? Is any unfinished business weighing you down and holding you back? Are you *willing* to lighten up and move forward?
- If there are walls you've erected or habitual stories you continue to tell, do they bring you up or down the Instrument Panel? Are you willing to soften your resistance and bring more attention to how you feel? Are you willing to tell a new story?
- When you are willing, The Divine can more easily do the heavy lifting.

▶ PLAY ALONG: *Nurturing Outer Connections*

The small self sees everyone as separate from it. The Large Self knows the interconnectedness and unity of all life. This isn't something your small self can understand, logically. It can only be experienced. You experience it more and more as your vibration rises and you move towards the experience of your Large Self.

- Bring to mind a relationship where you feel some distance—where you want to feel more connection.
- Rather than making anything wrong, or blaming either of you, experience how this separation feels *in you*.
- Perhaps it currently shows up in the form of *fear, sadness, longing, anger, blame, worry* or *frustration*. Maybe it shows up in the form of burning through your chest, a gnawing in your gut or tightness in the back of your head when you think of this person.
- Here is the magic: when you choose to pause, soften, and meet *yourself* wherever you are, no matter what you are feeling, you automatically step into greater connection—and this ripples out into your relationships.
- **You don't have to fix the condition of separation; you just need to build a new habit of connection.** You do that whenever you meet yourself in The Presence. In The Presence, you experience the wholeness and connectedness implicit to your being. Living from greater wholeness and inner connection, you naturally soften into greater connection with others, increasingly seeing and experiencing them through Large-Self eyes.
- Compassion, understanding and empathy flow naturally from a Large-Self perspective. In fact, true compassion, understanding and empathy for others are not possible until you truly experience this inner connection and communion with yourself.

At a certain point, your life up to now
will make perfect sense.
In the meantime,
if what's happening now doesn't make sense,
find ways to feel good.
Feeling good makes sense now.

PLAY ALONG: Reclaim Responsibility—And Power!

When you make other people responsible for your happiness you give away tremendous power and attract people who may exploit this vacuum of power, consciously or not. People respond to the vibration you're broadcasting. When you broadcast "being a victim," you attract people who treat you that way; people in your life arrange themselves to fit into your particular vibrational puzzle. From a truly Large-Self perspective you can see that it's not personal; they're not bad—they're just showing you how *you* are vibrating. But it can take a bit of practice to live life from such a wide perspective, and no one does it perfectly all the time. Nevertheless, it is possible to see anything that happens as an opportunity to clarify and manage your vibration.

- Seeing yourself as a victim may have a lot of momentum behind it. You may have collected a lot of evidence that supports it. But if *you* want to determine the course of your life, it's time to claim your power and responsibility.
- Where do you forfeit power and allow others to determine your wellbeing? In all your relationships, are you happy no matter what the other person is doing? If not, you are allowing others to determine your wellbeing.
- Intend to notice this week when you slip into victim mode. Don't judge, just notice. How does it feel? Is there a certain power in that stance? Is it true power or does it fade and feel sticky, messy or manipulative? Does it nourish or does it leave you always starved for more?
- True power has nothing to prove and doesn't need approval from anyone else. It isn't manipulative. True power stands on steady legs and speaks loud and clear without ever raising or diminishing its voice. True power takes responsibility for itself.
- Nothing increases power more than taking full responsibility for yourself and your life—even if you don't know how you're creating it! Soon enough you will.

❖

Allowing For Greater Health

Your health reflects your vibration. As your vibration rises, health conditions often improve, sometimes dramatically. This has been true in my life.

Health problems occur when energy isn't allowed to move. When you resist feeling and make certain emotions scary or wrong, you don't allow them to rise in vibration. The unwanted vibration stagnates and hardens but nevertheless still vibrates and eventually manifests in the world as an unwanted situation or perhaps a health issue. Divine Openings can interrupt and reverse this process.

Grace can heal an ailment that has already manifested, shift and improve outer circumstances, and get old, lower vibrational energy moving so that your point of attraction rises. You must support this process, however, primarily by owning your power, managing your focus and being willing to let energy move!

Health and wellbeing are natural. Their absence simply means you have picked up vibrational habits that aren't working for you. But habits are changeable. Let Grace help you change them.

"A dis-ease is a vibrational condition;
it's not really a 'thing' until we name it, diagnose it, focus on it, and make it so.
It can be interrupted at any level.
Divine Openings interrupts it at a very high spiritual, vibrational level,
and then the body reorganizes and restructures.
Again, don't resist—choose ease."
Lola Jones

⏸ PAUSE AND REFLECT on Your Stories About Illness

For people vibrationally attuned to consensus reality, illness can become a perfect opportunity to reinforce *fear*, *powerlessness* and the belief that struggle and suffering are normal. They tell *frightening*, *disempowering* stories, often see themselves as victims, and end up celebrating drama and hardship. They don't realize that observing, describing, reporting and complaining is *creating* more of the same.

- If this is your habit, relax. It's really okay. Just intend to notice where you are giving power away and how you feel when you do. Remember, awareness naturally loosens and relaxes old, engrained habits and allows Grace to raise habitual, sticky vibrations for you.
- Pay attention to the stories you tell and acknowledge the airplay you give unwanted things in your life.
- Do you share every detail of your lack of wellness with others?
- Do you form and join groups where the main purpose is to reinforce and communicate struggle, suffering and powerlessness?
- Does your lack of health in some areas blind you to your health and wellbeing in others?
- Consider taking your stories and worries solely to The Presence within.

⏸ PAUSE AND REFLECT on Being Curious About Pain

When you identify with pain ("I am my pain"), label it ("pain" instead of "burning," "throbbing," "stabbing," "pounding," etc.), or believe scary stories about it ("it's never going to end"), you inadvertently help keep it in place.

- If you have pain, practice experiencing the pain as sensations in the body and get curious about them.
- Curiosity is neutral; it doesn't grasp or define. Its lighter touch allows things to shift.
- Sensations are constantly shifting; if you give them your active attention, you will notice that your pain is not a static thing.
- How could you soften into *Yes* around pain? Just a little softening goes such a long way.

Recently I found myself in significant (and familiar) pain one night. In the past, this pain was a precursor to a chronic condition flaring again. This time, I noticed I was making the experience wrong and trying to figure out *why* it was happening. So I intended acceptance (simply because it *was* happening) and decided to temporarily put aside all the stories that were beginning to brew.

The relief was immediate and palpable. Resistance in any form always adds to pain, so when I removed it, my pain lessened. From this bit of increased relaxation I could more easily bring an active, deep interest and curiosity into my body, and this created even more inner space for physical and non-physical vibrations to move. Present, open curiosity lightens anything it touches. Try it.

In the morning, I awoke pain-free. Things like this happen all the time since I started in Divine Openings—not every time, but more and more as I learn to let go and allow them to.

"I want *this*" is always more powerful than "I don't want *that*."

"I want *this*" is always more powerful than "I don't want *that*."

▶ **PLAY ALONG: Find Things To Appreciate**

Every situation or condition reflects where power is flowing more freely or where energy and power is tied up. Stepping back and understanding from this perspective helps you appreciate the messages, and appreciation helps them move more easily.

- If you have a health condition, try to find appreciation for the information it is providing. Appreciation feels good and raises your vibration.
- Appreciate moments of greater ease and deliberately soar there! Allow the desire for greater health to emerge naturally from these better feeling moments, rather than from fear or lack of wellbeing. "I want *this*" is always more powerful than "I don't want *that*."
- Allow this easier, more relaxed vibration to create a new matrix of greater health and wellbeing and let The Divine fill in the details. Then let yourself be pulled morewards.

▶ **PLAY ALONG: Get Help And Get Relief!**

Grace flows easiest when you are soothed and relaxed.

- Explore ways you can experience relief, comfort and ease. Appreciate and find relief in whatever way you can.
- Medical intervention can offer great relief! By all means, get it if you are guided and appreciate the profound help it can provide. However, don't give *anyone* the power to wholly determine your health and wellbeing. *Choose* how much of any "reality" you allow into yours.
- Some Divine Openings Guides offer healing sessions and have profound results.
- As always, listen to your inner guidance. It could come in the form of new information from a magazine you just happen to read, a casual conversation with a friend, a sudden interest in a nutritional change, or simply an intuitive knowing that this supplement or that practitioner would be able to help. I've received life-changing health guidance in each of these ways.
- As you become more attuned to your Instrument Panel, your ability to discern what's true for you becomes more fine-tuned—you can instantly feel which path brings you into alignment and which path takes you further away from it.
- If there is something too large for you to handle, you can always hand it to The Divine. Your Large Self is more than capable of handling whatever you surrender to it.
- And sometimes… no matter what one does, an illness remains. As with anything, if you don't make it wrong, you won't suffer. It is possible to experience peace in the midst of illness.

Expanding Into Enlightenment

Enlightenment is simply you waking up to the Larger part of you. It's a return to your natural, magnificent state. By Grace and intention, your focus and perceptions change and you begin to experience what was true all along. From this expanded awareness, life around you changes, often in miraculous ways.

*"The Creator is not complete, finished, and perfect waiting for us 'defective ones'
to get it right, redeem ourselves, cleanse ourselves, or be good so we get rewarded.
We are the Creator's adored physical extensions, bringing this physical dimension
more into alignment with the spiritual dimensions, just by being joyful, loving, and creative.
Isn't it a relief that it isn't work? Heaven on Earth was here all along;
it just takes awakened eyes to see it."*

Lola Jones

Each rise in elevation is exhilarating, though in the beginning it can feel slightly unsettling while you acclimate to the higher altitude. As your body adjusts, you do acclimate—because this *is* your natural state!

When you enlighten, you are literally lightening up. You are releasing old habit and beliefs that no longer serve and letting go of resistance to how things are. You are dropping burdens that have kept you weighed down and in opposition to the direction you wanted to go—which is always up.

The more willing you become to let go, the more quickly you move into harmony with Life—and the easier things get. Life can orchestrate the fulfillment of your wants and needs and move you effortlessly in their direction. The question always is: are you allowing it to?

⏸ *PAUSE AND REFLECT on Enlightened Math*

You don't need to struggle to figure out an answer to "the enlightenment problem." In Divine Openings, the math is easy. It's not the kind of math you can learn or understand with your mind; it can only be experienced. It boils down to this:

You, Exactly As You Are + Now + Yes = What You Have Been Seeking All Along

- There is an enlightened master already within you. You do not need to add more, do more, or prove yourself to it—it's already whole and complete. You are already whole and complete.
- Do you still feel you have to add or subtract something before you arrive?
- Consider that there's no subtraction in the Universe! It's all addition; it all expands you!
- Further, consider that there is nothing you *have* to add; you are whole and complete now even though you will expand. Enlightenment is not an end; there *is* no end! Expansion is an essential, integral aspect of Life!
- When you commune with The Presence within, you experience these truths, and you experience your wholeness. You can experience them now.

⏸ *PAUSE AND REFLECT on Seeing From An Enlightened Perspective*

When you're grinding on a problem, it's a sure sign you're stuck in small-self perspective. Sometimes all you need is a small shift in perception.

- Consider an area of your life where you would like more ease, movement and change.
- Acknowledge your feelings and concerns: perhaps there is *discouragement, worry, confusion,* or a *stressful* attachment to things working out a certain way. Feel how this gripping or grasping feels in your body.
- Now imagine your Large Self considering the same situation. Is there worry, stress or anxiety?
- If there are vibrations that need to move, by all means—let them move! Nevertheless, tapping into the non-resistant power of your Large-Self perspective can offer a helpful boost.
- You are free to step into this enlightened perspective at any time!

*"**Divine Openings** causes a moment of birth
—there's a crossing of a threshold into enlightenment,
and yet it is never quite 'finished.'
The entire universe is expanding, and so are we."*
Lola Jones

◐ **PLAY ALONG: Let Unworthiness Rise**

Holding onto unworthiness delays awakening. You spiral into worthiness choice by choice. Every decision to pause and go inward; each time you choose not to heed the "earn this" and "prove that" directives of mind; each gift of self-acceptance; and every gentle *Yes* you bring to your deserving softens the barriers between you and the remembering of your worthiness. As the barriers of unworthiness come down, what remains is your natural state, which has always been worthy.

- Right now you can step into a more empowered, worthy, self-assured and self-determined life. Step by step, this is how you evolve, eternally. Sometimes the steps are small, though sometimes a single step changes everything.
- You can take one of those steps this moment. Are you ready?
- Stand up and feel into your *Yes: Yes* has a relaxed, solid stance, powerful legs, open hands, a soft smile, and an accepting, knowing, eager heart.
- Purposefully, with passion and presence, take a step forward, and then another, into this more certain, powerful reality. Feel it. Claim it!
- Intend to speak to someone today from this perspective. Notice how it feels to be fully present in your own skin *and* able to see and take them in. Intend to live more often from that sacred meeting place between you and the world.
- There is never a need to subtract from oneself when meeting another, nor is there a need to subtract from the other so you can be yourself. Every meeting can only ever increase Creation, so begin to think only in terms of addition!
- Embody the inclusiveness of *Yes!*

◐ **PLAY ALONG: Design Your Enlightenment**

People bring various expectations to the experience of enlightenment. In truth, it is a very natural, normal process. Still, you get to design your own experience.

- How do you want it to unfold? Do you want it quickly or do you want to savor every step more slowly? (And remember, it never is finished!)
- What do you want? More peace, ease and freedom in your inner world? Better relationships, flashy outer experiences, or more power in the outer world?
- Think about this. Feel into it. Be specific. Write it down.
- It's best to know what you want, and then let go and allow The Divine to orchestrate the details, acting when guided. Remember, things go great in your absence!

Yes polishes your inner reflection so you can begin to see who you really are.

Section Six Mantra: Just Say Yes

GRACE IN ACTION

Pause *here* often. Take frequent trips and tiny sips, *now*. Your reflection here is whole. Drink it in. Stand in the perfection of this moment and know that even though things can and will change, you in this moment are as you should be. This moment, reflected through the wholeness of Presence, cannot be broken, and you in it are not. Be filled from this unbroken, unifying experience. When you move back into life, do so having been nourished, embraced, loved and fulfilled.

If you're anything like me, you arrive here, initially, battle worn and weary. The world can be a hard place when it's not softened by our presence. If we wholly trust our reflection to its mirror, we will not see our whole truth. Only half the story is reflected there, shadowed by all the ways "no," "not yet," and "not me" keep us less than we are. My own eyes adjusted so well that I became quite acclimated to the shadows.

But by Grace, sight can be restored. As you pause *here* often, and take frequent trips and tiny sips, *now*, your own beautiful life comes more and more into focus and as it does, your place in the larger world becomes more clear. Every pause, every *Yes*, expands you beyond who you think you are. *Yes* polishes your inner reflection so you can begin to see who you really are.

Sometimes I still feel shattered, for hours, a few days or maybe even a week or more. If I look outward for my reflection during these times, I can easily become lost in the story of my brokenness—how I'm wrong for who I am, where I am, what I do, and how I feel.

But when I gather my shattered pieces together and gently lay them down in the soft place of my allowing, there can be acceptance for who I am right now. Acceptance allows me to see the beauty reflected in all my shattered bits. It softens sharp edges and makes them less frightening, allowing what needs to move, move more easily. Acceptance helps me tap into the wholeness that already exists, despite the seeming appearance of brokenness.

There is no fixing, nor is there any need. Life will naturally soften your rough edges if you let it. Can you find the willingness to stop using your broken bits and pieces to inflict pain and inner violence? That is the only request that Life makes, if you want to be carried by its loving flow. And it is a request that can only be answered here, now.

*"We straddle two dimensions——the older dimension
in which we have to massage our thoughts and feelings
to get them up or to keep them at a high altitude—
and the next dimension of life that is opening up,
in which our enlightened minds produce thoughts and feelings
of a very high altitude more of the time.
In the old world we had to work hard to force enlightened thought
because our brains were not wired to sustain it.
Now Divine Openings literally plugs us into our Larger Intelligence,
activates our higher capacities, and upgrades our systems
so that we can run 'enlightenment software.'
When we're no longer slaves to our thoughts and feelings,
nor unduly identified with them, it's easier to stay up.
We have still have Free Will choices, though."*

Lola Jones

Section Seven: Get Yourself To The Party

You Have Free Will

In Divine Openings, Grace does so much, but you still have Free Will and can support or thwart (though never completely) the Flow of Grace. *Things Are Going Great In My Absence* shows you how to make the most of your Free Will choices. I have distilled some of its guidance into mantras you can use in almost any situation: Slow Down And Show Up; Make All Feelings Good; Take It To The Presence; Go With The Flow; Choose Your Focus; and Just Say Yes.

Now you will explore more specific processes that give increased focus and momentum to your unfolding. Lola calls them the *"fundamentals of steering your life and manifesting your desires"* (page 99).

⏸ PAUSE AND REFLECT on Using Free Will To Let Go

If you want to let Grace do for you what you have been unable to do for yourself, you must choose to let go and let it. Letting go of old, unhelpful, obstructive vibrational habits happens naturally as you stop grasping and holding and pushing and pulling. Letting go can surely happen in your absence, but it more often happens in The Presence.

In an initial *pop* of presence—"Oh, here I am!" or "Ah, I am here..."—you cross the first threshold of letting go; you have already let go of resistance to acknowledging and showing up for what's currently happening. Sometimes you get there by choice and sometimes you just wake up in that larger, witnessing perspective. However you arrive, now you have choices. A powerful choice is to cross the next threshold into acceptance—to play with the possibility that "this should not be happening" can let go to "it is." From acceptance, possibilities emerge that you cannot fathom from lower vibrations.

- Whatever it is you want to release, it more easily drops away when you stop fighting it.
- Fighting against doesn't feel good. Instead of fighting against, decide to *be with*.
- There's so much to be with, right here. There's so much to love, now. Discover this truth.
- Be with whatever helps you feel better now. Fall in love with The Presence. Hold on to that.

▶ PLAY ALONG: Choose To Read With Fresh Eyes

In Divine Openings, Grace adds wings to your willingness and helps you fly in areas you were grounded before. But lift-off will be delayed if you are holding onto old ideas about how things are. Grace can't show you how it *could* be if you are holding onto how it's *always* been or will be.

- This section of *Things Are Going Great In My Absence* is overflowing with life-changing information. Your mind may want to rush through or protest that it knows all this already, especially if you've done Law of Attraction work in the past.
- Don't fight your mind, but don't give into its tactics either. You are not your mind! Choose consciously. Ask: "Am I absolutely, genuinely living this?" If not, perhaps it's worthwhile to slow down and give yourself time to really savor, assimilate and integrate this new material.

*"Raise your altitude just because it feels better
rather than because you want the guy, the girl, the job, the house, or the money.
Do it for you. Do it because you've decided feeling as good as you can in this moment is vital.
Your life will always be this moment, and if you are a little bit happier in this moment,
and this moment, and this moment, you change the trajectory of your life.
Maybe you can't manage outer circumstances, but you can* choose *how to* focus *in this moment."*

Lola Jones

A Brief Review On The Importance Of Feeling Better

No matter what you want—a better job, more money, a happier relationship or a more peaceful life—what you truly want is just to feel better in any given moment, and this moment always provides the opportunity to move in that direction. Focusing on feeling better right now is the key to manifesting the better feeling things you want to do or have. Feeling just a little better is transformational. Even a tiny bit of relief can begin softening the barriers between you and what you want and get you moving towards the party, where the presents are wrapped and ready! If your mind needs a reason to choose a better-feeling response, remind it that there's really no other sane choice.

You feel better when you stop pushing against any experience. As you become willing to pause and feel what is, you allow emotional energy to move, and this movement feels good. This movement of emotional energy is how you progressively shift a constricted small-self experience into a more expanded Large-Self one.

Remember that all emotions are the same Divine energy, just moving at different speeds. Emotional energy that is moving faster feels better than energy that is moving at a slower vibration because energy—Life—is supposed to move! As it is increasingly allowed to, and as your default emotional set-points move up the Instrument Panel, you come into greater alignment with your Large Self. How you feel lets you know how aligned you currently are, or aren't.

How you feel and what you're vibrating is always broadcasting into the world, manifesting and attracting what shows up in your physical reality. If you want your outer world to be better, you need to find a way to feel better inside. Moving into greater alignment with your Large Self always gets you where you want to go faster and easier than forcing change in the outer world.

⓫ *PAUSE AND REFLECT on How Feelings Are Never Wrong*

A feeling just is. When you judge it or make it wrong, you prevent it from moving in the direction of *better*. When you resist it, unwanted situations arise to show you where you are not letting energy move.

- Judgment turns an entirely appropriate "I don't like this" or "this doesn't feel good" into an utterly immovable "this is *wrong*." There is a huge gulf between the two. Can you feel this?
- Notice how your body feels when you make something wrong. Notice the physical work that occurs when you stiffen, contract, push against and hold back. Feel how everything stops!
- What feelings have you made wrong, or avoided, denied or tried to bypass? Does *despair* make you freeze? Does *fear* make you take flight? Does *anger* make you want to fight?
- Certain emotions will make you uncomfortable, especially when you are beginning to reclaim your Instrument Panel. That's okay! You can learn to tolerate a bit of temporary discomfort.
- Instead of freezing, fleeing or fighting, you can learn to feel and let emotions move. Divine Openings shows you how—and shows you how to soothe yourself while you are.
- When you are able to soothe and be there for yourself through any of life's inevitable challenges, you realize that challenging situations become...acceptable. This is huge! The reward is a permanent end to suffering.

It's not wrong to want what you want.
It's not wrong to do the thing that feels good.
It's okay not to suffer.
(Your suffering does not help the world.)

⏸ PAUSE AND REFLECT on *The Power Of Relief*

Each little bit of relief helps you feel better now, and this inner relaxation and movement is the key to generating outer movement. Relief is huge and always indicates you are softening and moving in a better feeling direction.

- Consider something unwanted in your life right now. How can you get a little relief *now* on the subject?
- Can you prostrate and turn it over to The Divine?
- Can you find a way to distract yourself from the story and focus on something else that feels better?
- Can you tell yourself a better story—that it's temporary and moving (which it always is as long as you don't resist)?

▶ PLAY ALONG: *Observe How Your Small Self Likes Bad News And Hard Work*

Your small self doesn't necessarily want to feel better. The small self likes focusing on problems! It enjoys telling scary stories! It loves having things to work on and fix! It literally lives to point out how you are wrong and then convince you that only it can make things right! It's not bad for doing this; it's just what small self does. Its control and vigilance has helped keep mankind alive for thousands of years, but you are now ready to thrive, not merely to survive.

- Start paying attention to your inner dialogue. Notice how your small self makes things (and you) wrong. Notice how often "should" and "shouldn't" litter your inner landscape.
- Observe without making small self wrong, and respond as best as you can without pushing against or judging. Treat your small self as your Large Self does—with gentleness and love.
- Witnessing this dialogue without reacting loosens its hold and lessened its power over you.
- If you're not sure whether your small self or Large Self is talking, ask this: How does it feel? If it doesn't feel good, it's your small self.
- Remind yourself that you do **not** need to believe everything your small self says. The trick is to recognize and then interrupt its often-persuasive tirades. We are so accustomed to trusting its bad news that in the beginning, we can feel wrong for ignoring it. We aren't!
- You do not need to feel guilty for *not* believing the worst news. It's okay not to suffer. It's okay to feel good. It's okay to make choices that feel good. It's okay to let Grace make it easy.
- If your small self is telling you (often urgently) that the world will end unless you do this or fix that—or even (if you are quite low on the Instrument Panel) that you've done something so awful that your world has already ended—try to remember that your Large Self is still there, above the clouds, loving you, holding you and inviting you to reach for any thought or feeling that feels a little better in that moment. Do this first, before acting or reacting.
- When you interrupt such a downward spiral, you make space for Grace to lift you. From even small elevations, things out there begin to look and feel completely different.
- Remembering your Large Self is still there—even if you can't feel it—can interrupt the spiral.

"First priority: to get your Altimeter calibrated, get back in touch with your body and your feelings. Notice during your day, 'I feel this, I feel that.' 'This is what I feel.' No faking. You are where you are. Don't make it bad and don't try to change it; let it be what it is."

Lola Jones

PLAY ALONG: Start Fresh And Lighten Up

For many, it feels like the small self voice *is* the voice of God. The old-paradigm concept of God as angry and judgmental still has a hold in Ancient Mind, which experiences the world through a low-vibration lens of separation, scarcity, fear and insecurity. Get very clear that God has no self-nature. The nature attributed to God reflects the consciousness of the person or people attributing it at any given time. Your consciousness is changing. Don't drag old concepts of God into your new reality.

- Try this: the next time you imagine God is judging you, stop. Deliberately remind yourself that the Large Self doesn't judge and is always thrilled to experience Life through you.
- Listen for its ever-present *Yes*: "Thank you for expanding Creation through this experience!!" You may feel it as a *whoosh* in your chest or the feeling of *ahhh* accompanying a deep breath.
- Lighten up!! Decide to join the part of you that already has. Get yourself to the party! It's fun there! The only thing missing is you!

❖

Understanding Your Instrument Panel

Your emotions exist on a continuum, ranging from *powerlessness* and *despair* to *ecstasy* and *joy*. The Instrument Panel is another name for this emotional continuum. Lola's representation of the Instrument Panel helps clarify the emotional experience and is ultimately intended to connect you with your *own* inner Instrument Panel. If you acknowledge and deliberately use it, it becomes a clear map for exploring and living at higher and higher vibrations.

When you manage your emotions, you become *the* conscious creator of your life. By "manage" I don't mean suppress, control or "deal with" in the traditional sense, where feelings are judged as *wrong* and either avoided and denied or processed and worked on. I mean that you learn to value the miraculous moment-to-moment feedback emotions provide and use this information to more deliberately get yourself where you want to go!

People get disconnected from their Instrument Panels in different ways. Some people unplug from it completely; they lose touch with how they feel. Others mistakenly turn it upside down, so good feels bad and bad feels good. It's not necessarily important to understand how or why you may have gotten disconnected; it's important to reclaim it now so you can stop flying blind.

Flying blind is how most of the population travels. The great majority of people believe that outer circumstances determine how they feel. Not only is this backwards, it is also the root of much of the *powerlessness* and *confusion* in this world: people don't understand why certain things keep showing up in their lives and why they are unable to make other things happen.

The truth is, outer circumstances always reflect what you are vibrating; your vibration determines your experience. When you see the world through this lens, you begin to understand what you have previously created, and how. You also learn to predict how near or far you are from letting in the things you actually want. Clarity increases as you move up the Instrument Panel.

When you take deliberate inventory
of what's right in your world,
you build momentum in that direction.
How many things can you make right *right now?*

Remember, the formula for creating is: you ask, it is given, you let it in. The vibrational essence of what you want is created instantly the moment you desire it, and your Large Self immediately starts experiencing the truth of its manifestation. The closer you move into vibrational agreement with your Large Self, the easier and faster you can let it in. The Instrument Panel shows you how near or far you are from being able to let it in by showing you how near or far from your Large Self you are currently feeling about a particular subject.

When you use your Instrument Panel, life starts to make sense. To make sure you do, print out several copies of the Instrument Panel at the end of this book and put them where you will see them!

⏸ PAUSE AND REFLECT on *Making Things Right*

The biggest obstacle to moving up the Instrument Panel and feeling better is resisting what you're feeling now and not letting it move. You resist when you make *this* feeling or *that* experience wrong. Develop a new habit! With practice you can acknowledge and eventually accept the inherent rightness in any circumstance. It just takes a little shift of focus.

- How many things can you make right *right now?!?* List at least five things you might normally judge as wrong: the cat pooped on the carpet; the roof leaks; your head aches; traffic's backed up; there's no time to breathe...
- Now notice how your mind immediately wants to solve these "problems."
- Instead of reacting to the circumstances, recognize that each circumstance is reflecting a feeling that needs to move. For example, "I feel absolutely *powerless* that the cat continues to poop on the carpet."
- Then shift your focus from what's "wrong" in the outer world to what's true and "right"—or correct—in your inner world: you feel powerless. There's a good chance that powerlessness is a well-practiced vibration for you that the cat is just drawing attention to (animals and kids are particularly awesome that way).
- Ask, "How does this shift in perspective feel in my body? Does it bring me up or down the Instrument Panel?" Even if what you're feeling doesn't feel great, it's usually a big relief to acknowledge what's true—and relief offers a bit of momentum in a positive direction.
- As you focus on and manage your inner state, the outer world begins to reflect these shifts in your vibration, especially as you move up the Instrument Panel. "The Tipping Point" (about halfway up) is where you begin to really experience more malleability in the external world.
- But even if the cat still poops for now, when you recognize and let your feelings about it move, you gain access to new ways of handling her *and* your own reaction. When thoughts and actions arise from acceptance of what's true—or "right"—at this moment, they are more powerful and effective.
- If something happens that you just cannot *not* make wrong, remind yourself that there *is* a way to make it right—you're perhaps just too entranced by the physical manifestation to make the shift at this moment. Be gentle. Life is compelling and it's not easy to reclaim our power from what's happening out there. Be easy on yourself. Only take score when the score is in your favor!

"Say 'yes' to the feeling. This helps you soften. You might say,
'I hate this feeling, but I will embrace it.
Power is tied up in it, and fully feeling it gets me my power back.'"
Lola Jones

- At a certain point, wrong and right will stop making sense. In reality, things just *are*. In the meantime, Life will flow so much more easily for you if you look for things that are right than getting stuck on things that are wrong!

⏸ *PAUSE AND REFLECT on Reclaiming Your Power Bit By Bit*

People who continually bounce between emotional highs and lows have not built a solid vibrational foundation by authentically moving through the lower vibrations. Because they ignore, resist, deny or rush past uncomfortable feelings and experiences, they continue to slip back to those vibrations. If you want to get off the emotional roller coaster you must be willing to start where you are and move up the Instrument Panel bit by bit.

- Look at the Instrument Panel. What feelings do you find particularly unbearable? The ones that are least tolerable are ones you've avoided. They also indicate where power is tied up.
- Are there Instrument Panel readings you gloss over and don't really see? This too indicates that you have likely bypassed these emotions. There's power to reclaim there, too.
- Emotional energy needs to move and when you bypass or resist it, your creative power is spent holding back the Flow of Life. When resisted feelings begin to move, your creativity multiplies.
- Where is your power tied up?

▶ *PLAY ALONG: Recognize Your Stories*

It is not uncommon for the small self to turn a perfectly good-feeling story into a potential tragedy: "It may feel good now, but wait until..." Or turn a delicious desire into a noose: "That's a cool thing you want. Too bad it's not here yet. You sure are a loser for not already having it."

- Several years ago I noticed a yard in my neighborhood that I found particularly beautiful—a stunning mix of vegetables, flowers, trees, rocks, and tall, waiving grasses. I loved how the yard made me feel, and I could tell that the person who tended the yard felt good while doing so. Appreciation, longing and desire welled up in me—which felt terrific.
- But I happened to notice how quickly this *Yes* morphed into a story that felt bad—that I was somehow deficient for not already having a more beautiful yard and that this deficiency could only be corrected by fixing my yard "problem." It felt like hard work and sacrifice would need to be involved.
- However, because I caught myself slipping into this disempowering story, I was able to bounce back to *appreciation* and *love* and the pure *Yes* of my initial desire. That's where I kept my focus, and within a year my own yard had transformed, without undo struggle and hardship. Yes, it required effort, but the effort unfolded naturally, easily and joyfully.
- This week pay closer attention to the stories you tell yourself. Start to recognize which ones bring you up the Instrument Panel and which ones bring you down.
- As you recognize them, record them here.

*"If you're low on the Instrument Panel on a particular subject,
your job is not to get to ecstasy about it today. That's too hard.
Your job is to feel just a little bit better today and a little bit better tomorrow.
You can do that."*
Lola Jones

▶ **PLAY ALONG: Get Moving!**

Emotional energy is experienced in the body and can only move through the body. You simply **cannot** get the benefits of Divine Openings if you try to do this in your head.

- At the bottom of the Instrument Panel is *powerlessness; powerfulness* is at the top.
- Move through the feelings on your continuum, starting at the bottom. *Embody them* and notice how your experience of power increases as you move up the scale, where energy is moving more freely.
- Really do this! If you have resistance, then get down on the floor and experience resistance!
- Intend to experience more in and through your body. Begin to bring more awareness to the ways you hold yourself, how you move, what you feel, and where you feel it.

Using Your Instrument Panel: Reaching For and From Better Feelings

Your current feeling determines where you experience yourself on the Instrument Panel in relation to a specific subject at a certain time. Where you are is where you are. Judging yourself actually prevents you from moving. Skipping over a "bad" feeling ensures you'll continue to revisit it.

The first step in consciously working with your Instrument Panel is to acknowledge where you are: in *this* area, in regard to *this* desire, *this* is how I feel. You don't have to like it, but if you don't acknowledge where you are, it's hard to deliberately move in the direction you want.

For example, if you want to feel more *enthusiasm* and *passion* in your relationship, it's vital to know you're starting from *discouragement*. Making the jump from discouragement to passion is too big: Law of Attraction is still in play, despite the boost you get from Grace, and if you don't explore and really open up the territory between where you are and where you want to be, you'll continue to be pulled back to your vibrational set-point of discouragement.

Depending on your own emotional habits and disposition, some areas (some Instrument Panel readings) will require more exploration than others. In some areas, you'll need to stop and stay a while, especially if it's a well-practiced lower vibration (we'll cover that in the next section). In other places, you'll be able to move more quickly. But in general, if you want to experience a consistent, lasting vibrational ascent, small, steady steps get you there. The Instrument Panel maps your route.

Once you've determined where you are on the Instrument Panel you can begin to explore ways to feel better. If what you're currently feeling isn't too sticky—if it doesn't have too much of a backlog of unfelt vibration behind it—you can often just reach *for* a better feeling one or two places above where you are.

So, from *discouragement* you can wonder: is there *blame*? Is there *worry*? You ask and then feel for the answer in your body. Note that blame and worry aren't necessarily "good" feelings, but they are a bit higher on the Instrument Panel and have a little more energy and momentum than discouragement. You are looking to feel better relative to where you are. This is the key.

*"Give yourself compassion for where you are.
Soften up on yourself and you instantly move up the altimeter."*
Lola Jones

If either blame or worry feels authentically true for you, pause there and allow yourself to now engage with this new feeling. Don't engage with your mind, in stories, but with your body, allowing yourself to feel the deeper textures of this new vibration. Don't reach any higher for now; give yourself time to explore this new vibration.

Reaching *for* a better feeling can be tricky from very low on the Instrument Panel. When you are stuck in *fear* or *despair* or some of the other lower readings, it can be hard to look away from where you are; like passing an accident on the side of the road, the scenery down there can be tremendously compelling. In these situations, you can often find relief by reaching back *from* a better feeling.

Rather than looking directly at what it is you are currently feeling and trying to find a way to feel better about it, consider something else in your life where you already feel greater ease. Soar into the feeling that experience gives, then see if you can reach back to include the lower, sticky feeling in this new, better feeling perspective. Reach back lightly; soften and allow the higher-vibration to expand and gently invite the lower vibration in an upward direction.

Don't struggle at this and don't force yourself to feel better; it's a game! If you don't or can't find relief from a persistent scary story or low vibration, walk away! Let go of the "problem" situation, do something else that feels better, and let The Divine do the heavy lifting.

And please don't forget: whatever you happen to be feeling at any given moment is neither static nor objectively true. It may certainly feel true *to you* in the moment, but truth is relative and changeable: you feel *despairing, ashamed, afraid,* or *enraged* (etc.) until you don't—*until the feeling moves*. When you let feelings move, your truth will change.

⏸ *PAUSE AND REFLECT on Practicing With Patience And Kindness*

When you are awake and aware enough to acknowledge and consciously engage with a feeling, you are engaged in powerful emotional alchemy. Your most gentle, kind and non-judgmental attitude provides the cauldron for this work. You move up the Instrument Panel, towards reunion with your Large Self, by learning to treat yourself *as* your Large Self does. Be patient and kind as you practice.

- Acknowledge where you are on the Instrument Panel and notice your reaction. Are you judging yourself and making where you are wrong? If you are, feel into what feels worse—the feeling itself or your judgment of it.
- You are meant to have all emotions: each of them is valuable and none of them are ever left behind, no matter how enlightened you become. Imagine how life might play out if you didn't feel *fear* or *anger* or *confusion;* imagine the chaos that could ensue if you weren't open to the vital messages, warnings and guidance and that all feelings provide! You don't have to act on all of them, but you do need all of your feelings!! Claim your Instrument Panel!
- For fun, watch movies or read books outside your emotional comfort zone!
- When you experience feelings you have previously judged, rejected, or otherwise resisted, you are reclaiming a part of your own navigational system. Have patience! You are expanding!

"'Truth' is not the issue here.
Where you are is 'true' only because you created it,
or you bought into a reality someone else created.
You made it true. It's temporarily true till you create something else!
You can now create something else you like and make that 'true.'
Changing your story about it helps you feel more powerful,
and feeling powerful creates powerful realities."
Lola Jones

> **PLAY ALONG: Reach FOR A Better Feeling**

When you have a general idea of what you are currently feeling about a particular subject, you can use the Instrument Panel to investigate if there's possibility for movement.

- First determine where you are in a particular area of your life and then look one or two places above this feeling on the Instrument Panel. Ask: "Do any of these slightly higher readings feel true for me right now?" Feel for the answer in your body.
- If the answer is *Yes*, pause there. Immerse yourself in this new vibration; get comfortable with it. Spend as much time as you need letting yourself acclimate to this new altitude.
- As you do, this feeling will begin to feel normal. When it does, once again look one or two places beyond where you are and reach for another, better feeling.
- Don't put a timetable on this; go at *your* pace. Different feelings will require more or less time.
- As you explore each Instrument Panel reading, you open up and reclaim new, vibrational territories. You're widening, paving and smoothing the way between you and your Large Self!
- Savor this connection and rave about improved pathways between you!

In the beginning, identifying how you currently feel may not come easy. It's like rebooting an old, neglected computer program: if your Instrument Panel has been turned off, it can take time, patience, and practice for it to come online again. Be patient, use the tools you've already received, continue listening to your body, and keep practicing!

> **PLAY ALONG: Reach FROM A Better Feeling**

Sometimes, it's easier to get ourselves to a better feeling place and then reach *back* to offer ourselves some relief.

- Is there a persistent, low vibration that you have been unable to nudge upward? Or something you've wanted that feels sticky or stuck?
- What you focus on expands, so if you cannot find a way to make this feeling or desire better, focus on something else that does feel good! As best as you're able, turn away from the "problem" and turn towards something that makes you feel better. Fill yourself with that.
- *Allow* yourself to lighten and expand. At some point, your expansion might be large enough to soothe and include your feelings of contraction.
- This is a dance, an invitation. Don't make it into work! Be light with your invite and don't expect a specific or definite RSVP.

Using Your Instrument Panel: Telling Better Stories

"Telling a better story" is another way of shifting momentum upwards on the Instrument Panel. A lot of stories are produced by the "wrong seeking" mind of the small self and take some form of "I feel *this* way because *that* thing happened." Characteristically, both *this* and *that* are "wrong!"

"When you indulge in stories about how you got there, whose fault it is, and how powerless you are to change it, do those thoughts make you feel better, or worse? The game is to soothe yourself and tell yourself a better 'story,' one that leads to even a slight rise in altitude, a few steps up the Instrument Panel. Easy does it. One step at a time is all it takes to create upward momentum."

Lola Jones

This is an incorrect, backwards understanding of how creation actually happens, but unfortunately, these habitual stories are compelling and keep us stuck, trapped and powerless to make real changes.

Reality *responds* to your stories and vibration, not the other way around, and reality is ever-changeable. The quicker you can reframe a fearful or troubling story, the quicker you will reclaim your power to create a better feeling reality for yourself. The key is to reframe the story in a way that feels better.

In most situations, you can almost always find a little instant relief by reminding yourself that *all* feelings and experiences are messages from the Large Self showing you where you need to let energy move, and that energy naturally moves up the Instrument Panel when you don't resist it or make it wrong. Notice how this story feels better and distracts you from the one that doesn't!

Here's another story that always feels better: all feelings and experiences are temporary. And another: all patterns and behaviors are simply vibrational habits that can easily change with willingness, focus, inspired action (your part—10%) and Grace (not your part—90%).

Telling better feeling stories and reaching for and from better feelings give you your power back. They help you feel better *now,* which is what you really want anyway. And they build momentum in a forward-facing way, towards your Large Self and towards the outcomes you desire. They are the vehicles that take you where you want to go. The Instrument Panel is your compass.

If you find that you can't easily shift your focus towards something that feels better, then you can truly embrace and dive into what you are feeling, which is covered next.

⏸ *PAUSE AND REFLECT on Feeling Better From The Inside-Out*

Most people assume that people, events and things "out there" cause how they feel. They've been led to believe that if they want to change how they feel, they need to change things out there. But this is a monumental drain of their energy and power. It's not always easy to acknowledge and consciously interact with feelings we've avoided in the past, but it's much easier to acknowledge and move energy inside than trying to change things out there! Lola calls that "pushing rocks uphill." Let it be easier. Question your stories, let your feelings move, reclaim your power, and watch the world shift around you.

- The next time you notice that you're trying to feel better by changing something in the external world, pause. Ask: "What am I feeling?" Look on the Instrument Panel. Feel for it inside your body.
- Remind yourself that the vibration is creating your experience in the outer world, not the other way around.
- See if you can find a way to soothe yourself and feel better: tell a better story, or reach for, or from, a better feeling.
- Or, go for a walk! Pet the dog! Plan a delicious dinner! Hug your child! Hug yourself!!
- Repeat as needed. Notice what begins changing in your external world!

"Make the most of the best and the least of the worst."
Lola Jones

"Make the most of the best and the least of the worst."
Lola Jones

PLAY ALONG: Tell A Better Story

You can almost always feel a little relief about anything when you tell a better feeling story. Relief moves you up the Instrument Panel.

Continue to add to this list of better feeling stories you can use in any situation. Make sure you truly believe the stories you tell, not just with your head but with your whole being.

- "That scary thing out there is reflecting my vibration, and I can move my vibration."
- "All feelings are messages from the Large Self showing me where I need to let energy move."
- "Energy naturally moves up the Instrument Panel when I don't resist it or make it wrong."
- "All feelings are temporary, if I don't resist them."
- "No feelings are wrong. If I'm feeling it, it's right."
- "All current patterns and behaviors are simply vibrational habits that can easily change, with willingness and focus and Grace."

❖

Acknowledging, reclaiming, and using your internal Instrument Panel is the cornerstone of the Divine Openings experience. As you play with it, this experience grows and deepens. You discover your own style and rhythm. Eventually, feeling and navigating yourself up the emotional spectrum becomes so natural that you do it without even thinking about it.

Recently I became aware of a blindspot—a vibration of *guilt* around spending money on myself. I noticed the vibration while shopping for several social events outside my style and fashion comfort zone. Shopping for clothes has never felt good and this time was no exception.

What was different this time is that I *noticed* it felt like I was doing something *wrong*, and because I've learned to pause and investigate when I catch myself making things wrong, I was able to detect and shed light on this blindspot and not to buy into the story of my guilt. As a result, I could choose a different response. Noticing and allowing meant I could move the vibration.

Over the next few weeks, each time I noticed a fresh twinge of guilt I chose to relax into it. I didn't push it away, but neither did I let myself get sucked into its stories. My touch was light and bouncy, and rather quickly the vibration began to soften and rise.

What I discovered, deep down, is that I was *excited* to have opportunities to buy pretty things for myself and *appreciative* for the resources that allowed me to. Excitement and appreciation already lived in me; guilt had just blinded me to their existence! When we allow what's "wrong" to move, what's left is what's right! We don't have to create it; it already exists!

Moving up the Instrument Panel is natural. It is simply letting go of the small self's artificial barriers between who it thinks you are and who you really are.

Pause and truly feel the depth of your *more.*

Section Seven Mantra: Get Yourself To The Party

GRACE IN ACTION
You have been playing here for a while. Certainly, you are seeing evidence of Grace in your life.

And yet, possibly you want more... more awareness, better habits, a deeper opening to Grace, and more good "stuff." Maybe you want to live more often from the larger, more expanded perspective of someone who is open to Life—all of it. Perhaps you want your actions to more consistently spring from the conscious knowing of presence rather than from the often-unconscious thinking of mind.

Whatever desires have been building, your Large Self is right now experiencing the joyous *Yes* of their fulfillment. On a vibrational level, your desire for more is *always* met with *Yes*. The more deeply you get this, the easier it is to let go, act when guided, and allow *Yes* to show up in your world. The details of its manifestation won't always match your specific desire, but the vibration will.

So right now, pause and truly feel the depth of your *more*. Sense the width and breadth and weight of it. Feel into the state of being you desire. Let your stories about "how it hasn't happened yet" or "how it could never happen for me" dissolve in the right-now, white-hot heat of your longing. Feel this longing physically in your body. It is pulsing with life. Appreciate this focused, clear attention on what you want. This is what gives mass to your desire, pulling it into your gravitational field.

Eventually when "I want this" hits critical mass, it explodes into *Yes*. *Yes* aligns you with Grace. Implicit in *Yes* is "I choose this" *and* the enormously magnetic awareness that "*it* chooses me too." "I choose this" is your 10%. "It chooses me too" is Grace's 90%.

"I choose this" is your intention, blazing to life. Pure intent is dynamic; inner and outer worlds automatically reorient around this decision. If actions need to be taken, they flow more easily now—often effortlessly.

Bask in the glow of *Yes* and allow it to take shape. Let yourself be pulled into its current. Feel the Larger part of you calling you forward. Imagine stepping into this new reality. Choose to open into it, letting Grace expand and lift you along the way.

Feel the swell of power move through your being. This is Life, unresisted and true, pulling you onto its wave, into its Flow of power, reminding you of who you are and where you belong. This is you, showing up at the party and declaring "I Am Here Now!"

Intend with a soft certainty, expecting it to be easy and knowing that it's done. Then let go, trusting that your intention has been heard and affirmed. Now, simply act as inspired. Don't push; let yourself be pulled. Remember, "*it* chooses you too!"

So here you are. It is done. You have expanded Life with your focused desire and intention. Energetically, what you want already exists. You've sent a clear, vibrational invitation that Life can't help but accept as long as you don't contradict or rescind it. And now? Go party!

"With Divine Openings, The Divine does the heavy lifting. Grace does 90%. Your job, your 10% is to train yourself to use your Free Will effectively to manage your vibration, because Law of Attraction attracts feelings, people, things, and experiences to match what you are already vibrating."

Lola Jones

Section Eight: Drop The Story And Feel The Feeling

Life Isn't Wrong: Recognizing Blindspots

When unwanted things show up, they're reflecting feelings and vibrations you either avoid or have become blind to. Either way, they indicate where energy isn't moving. Grace gives a vibrational boost that helps things move, but Law of Attraction still applies and will pull you back into the density of vibrations that are particularly stubborn, resistant or simply not apparent. When you're blinded to a particular emotional pattern, you are less likely to question and shine the light of your awareness on it, so your responses are limited. My adventures with impatience (p. 39) and guilt over spending money (p. 135) are examples of blindspots coming into focus.

Blindspots are habits of vibration so ordinary and accepted that you don't notice them anymore. We all have them. Fortunately, Life always exposes blindspots by showing where you are out of alignment with your desires—where what you want isn't happening and unwanted things are. There are constant opportunities to question long-held, often hidden beliefs and assumptions that may be pulsing contradictory intentions, allowing you to move this old, stagnant, emotional energy. Whatever is happening out there, claiming that you created it—even if you have no idea how—is a powerful way to reclaim power, re-align with your intentions and create with greater awareness.

If surprising, unwanted things keep showing up or if there are things are not showing up despite using all the tools you're already using, it's likely you have a blindspot. Simply recognizing this possibility can often clarify and get energy moving, though sometimes it's necessary to get help from someone who isn't blinded by that particular vibration. Divine Openings Guides help with this.

Life does make sense. If you make what's happening wrong or make yourself a victim of it, you forfeit your opportunity to respond in thoughtful, productive ways. When you find ways to make things right and can take responsibility for them, you tip your nose towards better clarity, increased guidance and greater power to effect change. Always, from greater acceptance, you feel better *now*.

⏸ PAUSE AND REFLECT on Shining Light On Blindspots

We all have long-practiced vibrational habits that keep us stuck in undesired situations and patterns of behavior. It's okay. The less you judge where you are, the easier it is to turn yourself downstream.

Read through the following questions and note which ones feel true for you. Each corresponds to a place on your emotional scale. The ones that seem to pulse *Yes* show you where energy is likely stuck and creating unwanted outer events *or* preventing wanted ones from showing up. Don't judge; notice!

- Do you judge yourself or feel *unworthy* to have, do or be anything you currently want?
- Do you often feel *powerless* over people and situations? Do you believe you are a victim of bad luck and unfortunate circumstances?
- Do you feel you've done things that are unforgivable? Are you trapped in *shame, regret* or *grief*?
- Have you made the feelings of *hatred, rage* or *anger* wrong? Are you someone who never experiences anger or rage? Or do you frequently react with anger and rage?

***"Most humans keep looking at the unwanted thing
and give their power away to it, unwittingly feeding it their energy."***
Lola Jones

- Do you often feel *discouraged* and just want to give up?
- Do you *blame* other people and circumstances for things that happen or make others responsible when you feel bad?
- Do you *worry* constantly about your children, your spouse, or your finances?
- Are *doubt* and *confusion* default settings? Do you frequently wallow in indecision?
- Are you frequently *disappointed* by the things people do and say? By yourself?
- Do *overwhelm* and *stress* feel natural to you? Do you have trouble relaxing or doing nothing?
- Is *impatience* a constant companion? Are you frequently in a hurry to be somewhere else?
- Is your first reaction to things, "*no,* I couldn't possibly" or "that could *never* work"?
- Do you just *not care* anymore?

If any of these are true for you, and if life is reflecting this truth, celebrate the awareness. It's good to know where you are. Awareness brings fresh sight, clarity and new possibilities. From here you can go anywhere, and you now have the map and the tools to get there.

▶ PLAY ALONG: Claim "I Created This"

When something occurs in your life that catches you by surprise, it's indicating a vibrational blindspot you are probably not aware of. A feeling, thought or belief you have avoided, ignored or become blind to has attracted the outer condition.

- Recall a situation you were blindsided by: "The cat pooped on the carpet again."
- Acknowledge that *your vibration* is the primary causal factor. "Every time she does that now I feel completely *enraged.*"
- First of all, celebrate that *enraged* is higher on the Instrument Panel than *powerlessness,* which is how you felt the first time this happened! (Refer back to page 123 if you forget the incident!)
- Now get curious about the feeling: Are you frequently enraged? Can you soften and let yourself feel how rage lives in your body? Can you not make it wrong?
- (Don't make it wrong but don't *act* on it either: *"Negative emotion is for 'internal use' only!"*)
- Notice that the mind may want to understand *why* you feel so angry and *how* you came to feel this way. The mind tries to understand feelings rather than just feel them. Resist the temptation to follow it.
- Recognize too if the mind wants to make the cat wrong. "Yeah, but I'm enraged because the cat pooped on the carpet. If I fix the cat, I won't have this problem."
- The mind makes cats (and other things) into problems it thinks it can solve, deflecting attention from your true power and thwarting your ability to move the vibration.
- Saying "I created it" places you in the center of your power and allows you to move the inner vibration so the outer situation can shift.
- If certain feelings and situations consistently arise, there's simply a vibrational build-up (and a lot of stories) connected with that particular emotional pattern (rage, in this case). Appreciate the awareness and celebrate the outer indicators that show you where energy needs to move!

"You're always 'manifesting.' The key is to wake up to HOW you're doing it."
Lola Jones

You Are Creating Your Life

In this world, you are never simply observing, reporting or describing what's happening; you are creating it. You are always manifesting something! You become a conscious creator when you know how you're doing it. You may not always know the specific details of how a situation was created, but you can be certain that your vibration is always at cause. As you learn to intentionally move up the Instrument Panel into vibrational resonance with states you desire, you become able to consciously and deliberately attract the vibrational essence of what you want into your life.

You won't be able to always plan the precise route this manifestation takes in the physical world, the exact form it'll take (you'll know how it will *feel*), or how long it may take to get here. Generally, things manifest quickly with Divine Openings—especially as you move up the Instrument Panel. But your Large Self is at the controls and for many reasons, sometimes the path to what you want is filled with twists and turns you cannot understand from your small-self perspective. If you stay focused on where you're going and not on the current lack of it, getting there will be a more enjoyable process, regardless of how long it takes or how many detours you experience along the way.

PAUSE AND REFLECT on Not Taking Score Too Soon

"Don't take score unless the score is in your favor" is one of my favorite Lola sayings. It's a perfect, light-hearted reminder of the importance of focus and of feeling good! It's essential that you choose your focus and that you focus on what soothes and feels good. Focus on what *is* working. Focus on what helps you get there. Let everything else go. The better you feel, the faster it will come. It's really okay not to give attention to every single thing your "reality" is currently reflecting!

- When what you want hasn't shown up, what is your default response? Do you soothe and remind yourself that it's already created and coming?
- Do you use the Instrument Panel to pinpoint where you might be stuck or sending out contradictory messages, and play with ways to unstick yourself?
- Do you find things to appreciate along the way? Or do you take score and mark it as a "loss?"
- What feels better?

PLAY ALONG: Exercise Your Power Of Attention

You are always creating something; what you focus on expands. Consciously exercising your power of attention is necessary and empowering!

- Is there something you would like to happen today? How do you want to feel when it does?
- Don't pick something ginormous; just think of something that would make your day feel a little better.
- Now, can you *think* of it without contradiction? Can you stay with the story of "it's coming?"
- Can you *feel* into its completion with certainty, knowing it's already created?
- Can you do this for several minutes at a time? Try it!

*"By Diving In, I'm not talking about diving into the 'story about the feeling.'
The story gets you stuck, and generates even more of the unwanted feeling,
like running on a hamster wheel—you'll actually feel worse.
Drop the story;* feel the feeling itself."

Lola Jones

Diving In

If you repeatedly try to reach for a better feeling, tell a better story, or hand it over to The Presence but keep bouncing back to the same feelings and recreating the same old outer experiences, there is likely an old, well-practiced vibration that needs more help in moving. This is when you dive in.

Diving In is not clearing or fixing. Although it is a kind of process, it is not "processing" in the usual sense of that word. Diving In is simply a natural way to let stagnant energy move. It's how most kids deal with feelings until well-meaning adults train them out of it.

With Diving In, feelings don't heal or vanish; they move to a higher vibration. Feelings change state and lighten the same way ice thaws and changes form—from solid to liquid to vapor—progressively lightening and rising. In vibrational terms, as energy moves and changes states, you feel better.

Diving In works at the level of vibration. Diving In takes you past any story about *what* you are feeling, *why* you are feeling this way, or *how* you are justified in feeling it and moves you directly into the feeling itself—the actual physical sensations of the feeling in your body. Stories keep vibrations alive; diving directly into a vibration allows it to move.

When first relearning this natural process, it's okay to get started by gently bringing to mind a specific story or situation that seems to indicate where energy is stuck and needs to move. You do this only long enough to activate the underlying vibration. Then, as best as you can, you "drop the story and feel the feeling." All emotions have their own specific physical vibration, so you "feel the feeling" by sinking into the actual vibratory sensations you are experiencing in your body. Like slipping into a warm bath, you immerse yourself in your physical experience. The warmth is your kind, soothing, accepting awareness; you dive in with tenderness and gentleness.

As you submerge into your body, sometimes there is direct awareness of emotion: *sadness* is present, or *fear*, or *anger*, etc. Sometimes there are only sensations: the heaviness in your belly, the squeezing through your chest, the pulsing in your head, the clenched hands or breath, the heat or coolness or numbness. Sometimes there is an overall feeling of anxiety. Anxiety accompanies that often ubiquitous sense that your survival is threatened; it can be a general background fear that you are not safe in the world or a more specific response to an experience you are having. Your resistance makes it worse. Anxiety is always an invitation to pause, soften, soothe, and feel the fear that is present.

No matter what arises, your intention is to allow it all. There is nothing to figure out or clear. You simply acknowledge the feelings and sensations and allow them to be. This in itself is often a great relief. Just by letting go and stopping the impossible effort of pushing against what is, you relax.

People sometimes believe that if they dive in, the feeling will last forever. There's traction to this belief because in the past, feelings have stuck around—but only because they *haven't* been felt! With Diving In, you embrace feelings consciously, and your focus and intention invite movement. Soon enough you experience how emotional energy really does move and rise, when allowed to.

Diving In is different from other therapies, modalities and techniques in that you don't need to revisit or "heal" every wound or past event, one by one. Diving In moves things *en masse!* It raises an underlying vibration and unhooks you from its charge. This change ripples forwards *and* backwards;

*"Practice Diving In it until it's your new automatic response to lower vibration,
until you can catch a story before it gets revved up and takes over.
Even after you've been happy for years, sailing along on a steady high,
if your vibration plummets, the first reaction of the mind will probably be to make it W-R-O-N-G.
The story is, 'I should be beyond this now. I shouldn't feel this way.'
Making it wrong only compounds the resistance and prolongs your suffering.
As soon as you can gather your wits, make it 'right,' dive in, value the message of those feelings,
and experience them fully, you will rise, even from deep depths."*
Lola Jones

past events that carried the charge of this vibration no longer trigger or concern you. It's not that you've healed them; you've just allowed the underlying vibration to move and the situation now feels different to you. When things move, you feel better!

Diving into the direct experience of any feeling with your most tender, yielding attention soothes, softens and loosens old knots of solid, stagnant vibration. You not only feel better in the moment (usually) but as vibration rises, you also lift your overall point of attraction. With practice, you learn to embrace any feeling, at any moment. You come to appreciate their guidance and the opportunities they provide to reclaim power and free you from the habit of holding on to things that don't feel good.

Life is always providing contrast, and there are always things that will make you *sad, angry, discouraged* or even momentarily *depressed*, etc. But as you get comfortable with emotional energy and allow yourself to experience it in the moment, those feelings move—usually quite quickly. In Divine Openings, of course, this movement is smoothed and anointed by Grace. And like Diving In, Grace too moves things en masse—in your absence!

⏸ PAUSE AND REFLECT on Befriending All Your Feelings

Diving In allows old energy and lower vibrations to finally move, once and for all. It isn't done in order to get rid of an emotion but instead to befriend and reclaim your power from it. Your most feared, avoided and unwanted emotions are simply parts of you that have needed your acknowledgment and acceptance. When you can offer them what they want, they relax. In vibrational speak—they rise. When you don't fear any emotion, you are free (*freedom* is an Instrument Panel reading, by the way).

- Have you ever witnessed a young child in total meltdown? It's an extraordinary example of the power of feeling. It can certainly be intense, but if not resisted, the feeling always moves. Kids know this intuitively.
- It's interesting, however, to notice how adults respond. Most times, the adults try to squelch, deny, make wrong or otherwise resist letting that feeling move because such intense feeling makes *them* uncomfortable!
- The next time you see a child in meltdown (maybe not your own at first), notice how the adults respond. Common reactions are *shame, fear, anger, discouragement, disappointment, blame, worry, overwhelm, frustration, irritation and impatience*. These reactions always say more about where the adult is on the Instrument Panel than what is actually happening with the child.
- Pay attention too to your own response. Be curious! It's good to know where you are! It sheds light on your current level of resistance to or acceptance for your own often-intense feelings. Remember, the greater your acceptance, the easier and quicker things move
- At this moment, what are you feeling? How lovingly can you acknowledge and be with yourself, no matter what is going on?

"This is going to hurt" or "Through here, my freedom lies."
Which feels better?

▶ PLAY ALONG: Dive In And Be With It

Although Diving In is given as a formal process, it's really just the natural method whereby emotional energy is allowed to move. It will become more natural as you practice it. As I said earlier in this book, it helps the small self to break things down into multiple linear steps, but really, there's just *one* step: allow what's happening *now*. Do consider getting the Diving In And Being With It Audio Set to support your learning. When you can actually hear and feel how it works, vibrationally, the process becomes more accessible.

- If there is a present or persistent feeling or vibration that you'd like to move, dive in now.
- The attitude you bring to Diving In helps shape your experience, so observe how you feel before diving in. Notice how your body responds to each of these statements: "This is going to hurt" and "Through here, my freedom lies." Which feels better? Go with that!
- Diving In is a physical process. You attend directly to the sensations of a particular vibration in your body.
- If you are currently experiencing *fear* around money, feel the physical sensations of your fear, not the myriad stories you can tell about it. Feel the heaviness and pressure, the knots in your stomach, the catch in your breath, the sweaty palms and rapid heartbeat. Turn up the volume on the raw, vibrational essence of the feeling and sink into it—*as gently as you can*.
- You might not know what you are feeling in words; you may only have access to the sensations. That's fine! It's the experience that's important, not any word or mental concept.
- If there is a specific word that seems to describe how you feel, however, allow the word to settle into your body. Don't grasp at it with your mind; hold it softly and let it disperse and integrate into your physical experience. The word is not *it*: what it points to is it. What it points to are the feelings and sensations in your body—the *direct experience*.
- Be curious about how you are feeling! Bring a soft, active interest to your direct experience.
- As you deepen into the vibration, you invite it to move. *You* don't have to move it; your acceptance and attention soften resistance and allow it to move—as energy is supposed to.
- Stay with this experience as long as you feel called. Notice how the sensations change; they will! Be curious about this!
- When you bring such gentle, active acceptance to any vibration, it softens and begins to lose some of its density. Those tiny "bits" of energy get excited by your attention! As they speed up, slower-moving, lower vibrations begin to vibrate at faster speeds.
- Vibrationally, this softening and quickening begins almost immediately; often, the sheer relief of stopping your resistance is instantly palpable. You might experience it as an increased sense of inner spaciousness. There might be a feeling of relief.
- Nevertheless, you won't always feel better right away. This is okay; it doesn't mean you did Diving In wrong! Remind yourself that things *are* moving vibrationally (they are). Don't add more resistance by taking score too soon.
- When you dive in with an expectation of a specific outcome, you limit the possibility of that occurrence. Change will happen, but not if you grasp for it. Your allowance and acceptance of things exactly as they are right now are the requirements for all lasting and sustainable change. It's a paradox that's helpful to make friends with.

"When you fear no emotion, you are free."
Lola Jones

- If things don't move as quickly as you want, let go as best you can and do something fun and nurturing instead. Let The Divine do the heavy lifting.
- Sometimes when people dive into an intense emotion, it may feel like they *are* that feeling, and this can be frightening, especially if there has been trauma in the past. If this happens, widen your focus. Try to step back and witness. Remind yourself that you are *having* a feeling.
- Expand your awareness to include your outer experience: feel your feet, acknowledge the support of your chair, of the floor, of Earth—and breathe. Invite your Large Self to be with you (do this anyway). Always get outer support if needed.
- If you find yourself resisting feeling certain lower-vibration feelings, don't add more! Don't judge and resist your resistance. Don't force it to let go (it won't!).
- Instead, dive in to how resistance feels! Really experience your inner *No*. It's likely a habitual vibration that needs your willing, accepting attention. See if you can embrace the opportunity to make peace with it. It *is* a part of you. Soften, open, and allow it to move, when it is ready. It will.
- Remember, there are good reasons you've avoided certain feelings in the past. Be gentle with yourself. As you become willing to feel any emotion, you reclaim all the various shades and tones of your emotional continuum, and when those feelings surface in the future (they will), they will move much more quickly.

Over the years, Lola has offered different variations of Diving In in courses and audio sessions on the Divine Openings website. I outline a basic structure of Diving In that has worked well for me and my clients. Play with it and discover what works best for you!

In time, you will be able to dive in to any emotion quickly and easily. As you become more comfortable with feeling and moving emotional energy, willingness and intention are all you will need to raise any vibration towards "Ah, that feels better." Remember, there's always just one step: allow what's happening right now.

▶ PLAY ALONG: Dive In And SOAR

Any feeling, deeply felt, moves you up the Instrument Panel. It's what energy does. It's natural.

- If you still need evidence that Diving In is not healing or fixing but instead simply allowing emotional energy to rise, find something to celebrate and soften into appreciation as deeply as you can.
- Relax into the deliciousness of this experience and let the *ahhh* of it infuse your being.
- Feel yourself open and allow yourself to rise, like a balloon expanding into even greater alignment with The Presence within.
- No matter where you begin, every feeling can move up the Instrument Panel!

Let yourself burn until the soothing waters come.

Section Eight Mantra: Drop The Story And Feel The Feeling

GRACE IN ACTION

It's a quiet moment and my mind has gone back in time, revisiting an experience that instantly brings the hot flush of shame. The discomfort makes it hard to breathe. My heart pounds and I wonder what I can do or who I can call—anything to fix this red-hot fire of humiliation and the naked truth of my awful imperfection.

I want to run from this feeling, or hide from it.

But I don't move. Even as sweat forms on my brow, I don't run away.

Instead, I turn from the story and lean in to the inner furnace, allowing it to burn. My shaky breath fans the flames. They blaze and rage and I feel I might be consumed by them. It's so hot and uncomfortable that I have to steady myself and offer soothing sips of tenderness: "Just breathe, it's okay, this is temporary, it's moving…"

And it does. The heat subsides, my breath returns and I've survived. I am transformed.

The story flows back into my mind, but now I can be with it without its fevered charge.

Yes, this happened.

Yes, I did that.

Yes, I can take responsibility, share my regret and make amends, if guided.

And *Yes*, The Presence still loves me, no matter what. It's true, and now I know it. Despite my human imperfections, I now bear the mark of a more perfect truth, branded by acceptance, sealed in The Presence: I am always loved and accepted.

With any fire fully felt, there are always the cooling waters that rush in as judgment recedes. You find comfort and relief in their wake.

Feel the fire, no matter how it starts. Hatred, fear, despair and shame, deeply felt, will burn. Let them. Give yourself to them. Trust the wisdom of the elements. Here, fire transforms, but it cannot destroy. Your surrender, soft and yielding, flows you back to the ocean of your truth.

Let yourself burn until the soothing waters come.

> *"What if this life (and The Creator itself) is more experimental, unfinished and adventurous than we believed and welcomes your help creating the future, giving you carte blanche to do whatever you like and eternity to try different things?"*
>
> Lola Jones

Section Nine: Take Time To Align

It Gets Easier

As your awakening unfolds, it becomes easier and more natural to manage your vibration. The conscious-mind tools that Divine Openings offers make sense; this becomes obvious the more you use them. You will always need to make smart Free Will choices, but increasingly, this happens automatically. Life continues to provide contrast, but you're less reactive to it and less compelled to fix outer states until you have greater vibrational congruence with what you really want.

When you appreciate the role of contrast and feel good in spite of it, you more easily bounce off it and towards things you want. Don't pounce on lower vibrations and try to fix them: bounce instead!

⏸ *PAUSE AND REFLECT on Making Up The Game AND The Rules*

As your vibration rises, you realize there's no preprogrammed Divine plan that you have to master and complete. Your "purpose," if there is one, is simply to create—and to enjoy yourself as you do! You are perfect now *and* evolving endlessly morewards, and *you* get to decide what more looks like.

- You cannot believe there is a Divine game plan you have to follow or fulfill without also fearing that you could be doing it wrong.
- But you can't lose the game when you determine the rules and how it's scored.
- You get to choose where you focus your attention, how you want to feel, what you want to do, and when you're ready to do it. And you get to choose when to take score (hint...wait to take score until the score is in your favor!).
- If you were really certain you could not do it wrong or fail, how would you live? What would you create? What do you *want* to create?
- Dream, without worrying how it could come to pass. Savor the expanding *joy* of dreaming.
- If resistance emerges (for example: *doubt* that it could ever really happen, *uncertainty* about how it could, *disappointment* that it hasn't already happened or *impatience* that it's not happening quickly enough), dive into that feeling, let it move, keep on dreaming, and act when inspired!

▶ *PLAY ALONG: Ease Into Your Body*

People who avoid or have become cut off from their feelings are generally also cut off from their bodies. You feel emotions in your body, so if feelings have been overwhelming or painful in the past or if you weren't supported in learning how to feel them, it makes sense that you might find ways to numb and check out of your body.

If this is true for you, be gentle with yourself. You didn't do anything wrong. On the contrary, without adult guidance to model conscious feeling, you took care of yourself as lovingly as you were able. And nothing is wrong now. This is the perfect time and place to reclaim your feelings, your Instrument Panel and your body: you have new information and you have support. You just must be willing to begin where you are.

Pleasure is always increased by presence!

If your body feels numb or frozen, then so be it. Let the authentic desire for more feeling grow from where you are. It will.

- Right now, **stop**. Pause and allow your attention to soften. Bring this softened attention into your body and inquire, "What am I feeling?" Scan for sensations. What piques your interest?
- When something does, pause and deepen there, simply for the joy of meeting yourself more fully. Notice the space created by your allowing.
- How does more spaciousness feel? What is filling that space? Is what's there static or does it shift and move? Do you notice how things *can* move once space has opened up? Can you let them? Play with this. Let awareness awaken your body.
- Another way to awaken the body is to purposefully bring attention to specific body parts. Begin with one foot, or even one toe. Soften into it and allow it to come alive: the same Life Force that flows through stars flows in that toe! Feel it!
- You can also follow your breath, notice the solidity of your hips, explore your shoulders, and inquire into your hands. Or, investigate and soften into each part of your head, face and jaw.
- Better yet—give yourself a face massage! Bask in this gentle, delicious self-care and attention.
- Being in a body was never meant to hurt or be a punishment. Fill it with presence and rediscover the *joy* of your human embodiment.
- Diving in to your body in this way is done purely for pleasure. This kind of "pleasure practice" makes you feel good now and softens resistance so Grace can help move things for you.
- You can make almost anything a pleasure practice if you bring your most sumptuous attention to your senses as you do it; walk and feel the wind caress your face; leisurely stretch your spine; savor a favorite food; share your touch with others; or simply show up fully the next time you are in the shower and really savor the experience.
- Tuning into your body is a helpful way to relax at night, especially when the mind is spinning. Attending to and softening into your body gives your busy mind something else to do and creates space to relax into.
- Bodywork is terrific for people whose bodies have become numb. Rather than zoning out or using the time to solve the world's problems, intend to consciously show up for the experience. Pleasure is always increased by presence!
- Additionally, in the Diving In Audio Set there is a "Body Scan" audio that is purposefully designed to help increase awareness of feeling in your body. Listen to it often if just for the joy that is possible when you meet yourself in any way.

What Do You Believe Is Possible?
The future you experience hinges on today's decisions. In each moment there are endless possibilities and potentials you can activate for yourself. You may have been trained to expect small. Here, you are invited to dream big! Remember that *you are creating it all*. This is a huge shift in consciousness.

The better you feel, the clearer you get.
Clarity feels like *Yes,* in your body.
It feels good.
Wait to act until you feel good.

Unfortunately, most of us have unquestioned beliefs and expectations about how the world works and what we think is possible. Over time we collect "boxes of evidence" that seem to prove these beliefs. We think our beliefs have formed as a result of this evidence, but really, the evidence—and our reality—conforms to our beliefs.

Life gives you evidence of what you believe. If you believe, like most people do, that unwanted things are normal and natural, you will experience the consequence of that belief. If you believe there's a limit on what you can achieve or receive, you will live out that belief. If you believe that "facts are facts," your reality will squeeze itself to fit inside those facts.

But facts change and reality is more malleable than you imagine. Grace is real and Life is on your side, inviting you always to expand in the direction of *more*. You create new realities each time you question old beliefs! You don't have to take my word for this! With Divine Openings, you experience it directly. As you reconnect to the Source of direct, in-the-moment guidance, you naturally expand out of your old, fear-based, limiting boxes and begin to live from greater freedom and possibility.

◉ *PAUSE AND REFLECT on Acting And Making Decisions From Greater Alignment*
Your Instrument Panel and your deepening relationship with The Divine are the two components of your internal GPS system. Truly, they are the same thing; when you acknowledge, reclaim and use your Instrument Panel, you are connecting with Divine Guidance. Your GPS gives you up-to-the-minute guidance about when to act and which choices will point you in the direction you want.

- How do you go about making decisions and taking action?
- If you make habitual choices based on what did or didn't work out in the past, your results will likely be stale and out-of-date.
- If you make hasty decisions from *uncertainty, confusion,* or *impatience,* your results will likely be muddy, unclear, and out-of-sync.
- If you react from *fear, anger, worry* or *irritation,* you will likely create more fear, anger, worry or irritation.
- ***If you're not present, don't have clarity or don't feel good, you are not ready to act.*** Habitually doing what you've done in the past, rushing into action, or reacting from lower vibrations ignores vital information your feelings are providing this moment.
- Pause. Look at the Instrument Panel and feel into your experience; acknowledge where you are and what you want now. If you are low on the Instrument Panel, find ways to feel better before taking action. Choices and actions should ideally be made when your feelings are more closely aligned with the outcomes you want, from higher on the Instrument Panel.
- If you're unclear, dive into your *uncertainty* or *confusion* and let it move before you act.
- It's a new world when you recognize there are fewer "have to's" than you thought. Yes, you pay the bills, feed the children and show up when you say you will. But many of the choices about what you do and when are much more flexible than you now believe.
- Take time to align. Allow your own authentic wants, needs and unique timing to emerge.

*"Now that your energy is up
and you're allowing the Flow of Life to carry you along,
you'll feel inspired to act.
Once you get clear on your true, authentic direction,
a fire lights under you, compelling you to take action.
You may be led to one step at a time.
Begin by taking one step."*
Lola Jones

PLAY ALONG: Notice Your Beliefs

It can be hard to recognize limiting beliefs when you are blinded by so much seemingly convincing evidence. Of course people judge your looks or intelligence! Of course this world is broken and needs to be fixed! Of course the government can't be trusted! Of course money is hard to come by!

- Start to notice what beliefs and assumptions you have been living from. This exploration can be absolutely fascinating if you don't make it into work or get hung up on fixing anything. Working on things keeps them rigid and heavy. Awareness loosens and lightens so Grace can enter and do the heavy lifting. Just be aware. Better yet, get curious!
- Do you still believe that things only happen through hard work, sacrifice and suffering? That life is about lessons?
- Have you accepted a limit to how much joy, success, happiness or ease you can have?
- Are you certain that the "terrible twos" are a nightmare? That teens are difficult? That reading is better than screen time? That calories, fats and carbohydrates are bad?
- Are there things you believe you must do in order to be healthy/wealthy/enlightened?
- Do you believe your awakening requires specific, step-by-step rituals?
- You're not asked to give up any particular beliefs. Just notice which ones seem too real to even question. Could you be willing to question them?!?
- Write about them here, intend to let go, and then move on. Things change in your absence!

❖

Acting From Inspiration

Ninety-nine percent of creation happens on the Non-Physical level. This doesn't mean that you don't take physical action, however. You came here to experience creating *in* the material world *with* your physical form. Divine Openings shows you how to optimize your physical efforts. When intention, focus and energy are aligned, you "cut your action to a fraction."

Nevertheless, swimming upstream is worshipped in our world. Struggle and suffering are accepted and celebrated as necessary and character-building. Listening for and following our own inner guidance are not.

And certainly, hard work, passion and challenge are essential for human growth. But suffering and struggle aren't. Suffering and struggle show you're working against the current—that you're not attuned to your own needs, desires, guidance and timing. This is wasted energy. When you are oriented correctly, even though we may willingly expend huge effort, none of our effort is wasted.

Although challenges and accomplishments that have the quality of ease may sometimes be judged or scorned, some will want what you have. If they do, tell them you've reclaimed your inner GPS then give them *Things Are Going Great In My Absence!*

In the meantime, keep swimming *with* the tide! Pause often, commune with your Large Self, listen to and follow your emotional guidance system, respect your own timing, determine your own pace, honor what makes you feel better, and act from joy and inspiration!

*"So, act, yes.
But get your altitude up
and point the nose where you want to go first
with your energy.
Otherwise you're flying into a headwind.
You can't buck the natural forces of the universe.
It just makes you tired."*
Lola Jones

⏸ PAUSE AND REFLECT on Feeling Compelled To Act

Action taken from low on the Instrument Panel is often an attempt to push past an uncomfortable feeling and usually produces more of the same. Nevertheless, sometimes we feel compelled to act.

- The next time you experience an anxious urge to act, pause and ask: "Is there something I am trying to avoid? What do I think this action is going to *fix?*"
- Maybe you feel compelled to shop when what you really need is to feel the emptiness inside. Perhaps you feel compelled to continue an angry, unproductive conversation when what you first need to do is reclaim power and clarity by letting your anger move—in private.
- If you can identify what you are avoiding, pause, dive in, and allow that vibration to move.
- If you can't necessarily identify the root of your compulsion, then dive into the push and pressure of your urge. Let that energy move before addressing the outside "reality."
- Get to better feeling place before you take action. Notice the effect this has on what you do and its impact in the world.

▶ PLAY ALONG: Allow Space For Guidance And Inspiration

Inner guidance and direction is always available, but it's easier to recognize when the mind isn't cluttered. Giving yourself time to pause and connect with The Presence—whether you call it meditation, consciously folding laundry, appreciating a tree, or gazing at the stars—helps create more inner space, making guidance and inspiration easier to hear. Pause and notice more often.

- When you are washing dishes, brushing your teeth, having your first beverage in the morning or lying in bed at the end of the day, intend to purposefully be more aware.
- Soften: notice what's going on inside you.
- Breathe: connect to the steady rhythm of you.
- Expand: notice what's happening around you.
- Allow your awareness of inner and outer to dance, play and merge into this I AM moment.

▶ PLAY ALONG: Let The Divine Do The Heavy Lifting

There are many processes Lola gives to help you relax, align, and experience more freedom and ease. At the top of the list? Let go, get out of the way, and let The Divine do the heavy lifting.

- Prostrating, making a God List or creating Dream Assignments are helpful when you feel stuck, overwhelmed, or uncertain about what to do next.
- If immediate action is needed, take appropriate steps as best as you are able. But most things don't have to happen right now. Notice what happens when you first allow Grace to soften your resistance, soothe your *impatience* and clarify your *confusion*.
- Letting go is a practice, but it isn't work. Can you feel the ease in allowing?
- What can you let go of today?

Allow yourself to become ready, willing and able.

Section Nine Mantra: Take Time To Align

GRACE IN ACTION

Stop. Feel what you want. Allow it to emerge from the inner flow of your being. Do not pluck it from the swarm of "have tos" and "shoulds" that surely dot your outer landscape. If your mind objects, remind if of all the times you tried, and failed, to do what it told you to do, or what it thought you had to do to prove yourself strong or smart or worthy. Be patient as your inner ear attunes back to the truthfulness of your own right-now reality, and let your desire emerge.

And when it does, still do not rush into action before you are ready. If your mind objects, remind it of all the times you forced yourself into unwilling action and failed because you were not yet fully aligned behind the forward momentum of your wanting.

I failed to quit smoking countless times until a wise person counseled me to stop trying so hard and simply intend for more genuine desire and willingness to grow.

I failed in the past because although quitting was something I thought I should do, it was not something I yet truly wanted to do. I failed because I hadn't allowed desire to grow strong enough to unite all my resources behind a ready, willing declaration of "*Yes*, let's do this!"

As it turns out, "ready" and "willing" are necessary companions of "able."

So this time, I intended desire and willingness to grow strong, and then I let go and simply showed up for the experience I was having. I inhabited (and enjoyed) my experience as a smoker and stopped making it wrong, knowing that presence plus acceptance always allow for greater possibilities, more Grace, and clearer, more powerful desire and willingness to arise. I didn't limit or decide *what* "should" arise; I just occupied the experience I was currently having, trusting that new desire, and the means for its fulfillment, would naturally unfold if I didn't resist. They always do.

As intended, a clear and powerful desire did emerge, and it did include an authentic desire to be healthier and less dependent on outer things. Within weeks, this desire had grown strong enough to unite all my resources behind the ready, willing declaration of "*Yes,* let's do this." I became able to quit smoking. I had my last cigarette and that was that. Quitting was easy.

When your inner reality wholly agrees with what you want in your outer one, magic happens. Take the time to align. Allow yourself to become ready, willing and able.

*"The farther into Divine Openings you go, the more you'll turn inward
for support and communion directly with The Divine.
In the early stages, though, don't hesitate to ask for support.
It may feel like you're unhooking from the matrix, seeing behind the curtain,
as you remember who you really are.
The territory is unfamiliar, and it puts us all outside our comfort zones,
but the help is there within and without."*
Lola Jones

Section Ten: Be Happy Now

Stabilize In Your New Reality

You are nearing the end of *Things Are Going Great In My Absence*. What's next? For most, the Online Courses on the Divine Openings website help maintain focus and momentum while they continue adjusting to living in higher altitudes. Right now you may be soaring. But until you are truly stabilized, it's easy to fall into old habits and back under the influence of consensus reality.

People who have the most dramatic and lasting results stay very close to Divine Openings for at least year or more and then check in often, as needed, to get (and offer) support, enjoy the community, and simply soak up the high vibration! Visiting the Divine Openings website and sharing with others in the community feels good!

Divine Openings is constantly expanding, and Lola puts new material into twenty web-based courses. The Level 1 Online Course is the place to start: Level 1 provides foundational material and new processes that support your elevation out of suffering. It is an extension of the material in *Things Are Going Great In My Absence*, with the added bonus of over 40 audio recordings of Lola giving one-on-one sessions covering a huge range of topics. Listening to Lola's voice is a powerful experience and offers a potent vibrational lift.

The Level 2 course takes you further into *ease* and *joy* and into the new paradigm beyond problem-focus. Level 3 is about assimilating and celebrating, and Level 4, "Jumping the Matrix," helps you truly unhook from consensus reality and increasingly occupy a world of your own creation.

Additionally, there are Online Courses focusing on Love and Sex, Enlightened Business, Kundalini, as well as nine specific "First Aid" Retreat Courses that focus on particular issues.

Lola also offers live 5-Day Silent Retreats on both the East and West Coasts in the United States and also in the U.K. and Germany. These 5-Day Silent Retreats immerse you in Grace and accelerate your awakening like nothing else!

Divine Openings works, and it works fast. Still, if you want the practical, permanent results that so many have already found, keep showing up until you feel significantly better. It won't take long, but it usually takes some time because we do live in a space/time reality. Give yourself the time. Give yourself the gift of stepping fully into your new, expanded reality.

You Are Expanding The Universe

After your awakening is activated or deepened by your first Divine Opening, everything not in resonance with pure *bliss* and *ecstasy* begins to move and rise in vibration, as long as you don't resist. As emotions are mastered and your mind relaxes its problem-focused grip, intention becomes your most powerful tool. With less blocking the way, synchronicity, guidance and inspiration occur naturally and your creations unfold more easily. You lighten up and are able to see and experience the beauty, love and support that were always there.

"You will always and forever be in that gap between your next desire and the physical arrival of it, because as each dream is fulfilled, you will dream up another one immediately. That is your creative, ever-expanding nature. Get used to being 'on the way to...'"
Lola Jones

And still...your wanting will never stop. Your desires are essential to the expansion of this universe! If joy and bliss fade, it only means that you've acclimated to your current reality and are now ready for more—which is normal and natural and necessary for the expansion of Life. When you are moving with the flow, you create endless challenges that feel good and expand you. When you resist it and ignore your inner stirrings, you create drama that feels bad and keeps you small.

You are not meant to stay small. It is exhausting to hold back the waves of your expansion. When you let go and align with their power, there is relief. Any relief is huge. Relief is a springboard for forward movement, a gateway to all expansion, and a sure sign that you are moving in a better-feeling direction. Relief indicates that you are moving with the flow, in that moment.

Being in the flow feels good. *And*, doing things that feel good moves you into the flow. Basically, if you want to feel good, you need to make feeling good a priority! At any moment you can pause and ask: "Am I enjoying what I'm doing right now?" If not, is there a way to bring more ease and acceptance into it? Do you need to dive in? Can you find a better story to tell? Do you have a moment to pause and reconnect with The Presence within? Is it possible to let go and do something else instead?

Each small rise in vibration and each lift of emotion elevates your experience up the Instrument Panel, and as it does, not only does wellbeing increase but your outer reality expands as well. New possibilities, inspiration, hope and motivation emerge that you did not have access to from a more contracted vibration.

Can you see that how you feel is *everything*? It doesn't simply change how you perceive your experience; it actually changes your experience. Every rise of vibration brings you more and more into alignment with the part of you that is wholly awake and fully aligned with the intelligent and loving Flow of Life. Every better feeling expands you into the greater truth and power of who you are. Life IS different from that expanded state of being.

The Divine really does care about every detail of your life. The essence of everything you want is already created. Your main jobs, from here on, are getting out of the way, allowing the manifestations to show up, and letting them in. Your Large Self is already there. When your relationship with The Presence becomes more of a moment-to-moment communion, you are there too, whether or not the manifestations have shown up.

⏸ *PAUSE AND REFLECT on Tuning Into Your Expanded Reality*
Authentic *hopefulness, excitement* and *joy* for what you want helps bring that desire into your reality. The good feeling shows that you have tapped into the vibrational fulfillment of your desire in the Non-Physical, and your vibrational attunement helps magnetize it to the physical world. When you can savor the time between the non-physical and physical manifestations (and that time will steadily decrease), knowing that it's already created and enjoying the growing anticipation, you have reached a high level of mastery and manifestation.

*"Enlightenment cannot and will not freeze your bliss
into a static state that stays the same for ever after.
That would be impossible.
Energy wants to move, life is change,
your Large Self wants you to expand and grow.
Use your Free Will to create new joys and fresh highs
rather than expecting the old ones to stay."*
Lola Jones

- Maintaining a positive, excited, forward focus helps things come faster. Do you ride the thrill of "It's coming"? Focusing on its lack slows it down. You get to choose.
- Whatever you desire, it is already cooked in the Non-Physical. Can you appreciate and enjoy now the trail of its heavenly aroma? Get still and you can smell it. Feel your mouth water and your stomach rumble with anticipation. Let it seduce and pull you forward.
- You don't have to figure out the details of how this meal will ultimately be served in the physical world. Get curious about possibilities you don't know about yet! Curiosity helps you vibrate you more quickly into resonance with them.
- If you start getting bogged down in details, turn it over. Remember, things go great in your absence! Be light with your intention and then get out of the way and go play!

▶ PLAY ALONG: Want More, And Be Happy Now

So much is really about being okay with what's happening right now. If it's happening, it's happening; resisting offers nothing helpful.

- Is something unwanted currently happening in your life? How can you make peace with it?
- Finding acceptance does not mean you like or condone what's happening. It is simply the most empowered place from which to initiate change.
- You can push against or you can bounce off and move forward. Feel the difference between the two: "This shouldn't be happening" or "Here I am. Okay. What could I do now?"
- Which one causes you to tense up and hold your breath? Which one allows relief, *positive expectation* and even *excitement* to flow?
- Decide that telling *hopeful, positive, eager* and even *passionately enthusiastic* stories is more important than complaining. Decide that it's cool to be *happy* and *optimistic*. See what happens when you want more and still choose to be happy now.

You'll Never Be Done

You are nearing the end of *Things Are Going Great In My Absence* and this *Playbook*, and your journey is just beginning. Your expansion will never end. Your awakening will never stop. You will never be finished. Your wanting and your *Yes* will forever widen. Can you celebrate the eternal movement rather than the arrival?

Sometimes expansion is preceded by a small dip as you encounter old energy that needs to move. It will move quickest if you don't make it wrong. As always, Grace will support whatever you choose.

As you continue to allow energy, desire and emotion to flow, as they once did, you will stabilize into higher and higher vibrations. If you experience momentary contraction, ask: "How wide can my arms be? How inclusive can my *Yes* become? How softly can I relax into the embrace of my Large Self?" Ask and then let go, and let The Divine do the heavy lifting.

"Make peace now with your ever-expanding, never-ending journey through eternity. Laugh at the old notion of ever getting somewhere, becoming perfect, or 'getting it all done.' You'll die with an undone to-do list, but since there is no death, it doesn't matter. You'll continue on."
Lola Jones

⏸ PAUSE AND REFLECT on *Endless Expansion*

It is difficult for the mind to understand, from each new swell of expansion, that what came before was not wrong. The linear mind cannot grasp the holistic experience of "perfect *and* evolving."

- I have a particular yoga practice that focuses on balance. I spend a lot of time falling. But each time I practice I find that I can hold the poses just a bit longer. Does that make my previous practices wrong?
- When you bump up against this paradox and want to judge and make yesterday's experience wrong in light of today's even-greater expansion, recognize that yesterday's experience and the desires that arose from it literally *created* today's new, more expanded reality.
- Everything is unfolding perfectly. But you can truly only know this in The Presence.
- Attend, fully, to the experience you are having today. Intend to find your balance, as best you can. You can only find it here, now.

⏸ PAUSE AND REFLECT on *What Works!*

This list Lola made is worth repeating in full:

"The people who get free and happy the fastest:

- *Let go of everything they knew from the past, and don't mix modalities.*
- *Stop seeking, enjoy life, and stick with Divine Openings, which points them within.*
- *Appreciate all feelings. Don't resist any feeling or make it wrong*
- *Take everything within to The Presence instead of talking about it to other people, whether friends or therapists. Stop trying to get someone else to make it go away or fix it for you.*
- *Stop telling their old stories. Period.*
- *Claim responsibility for their own reality, even when they don't yet understand how they created a particular thing. They say, 'I created it,' in a kind, compassionate way.*
- *Let go of control and don't try to figure it out intellectually.*
- *Make a powerful decision to stop looking to the outer world for validation or clarity.*
- *Commit without reservation to creating their own reality, and stick to that.*
- *Don't take score too soon. Focus only on what's working, not what isn't. Delete 'failures' and don't count them.*
- *Practice appreciation and rave daily.*
- *Read this book many times, letting in more of it each time as consciousness expands.*
- *Stop working on themselves, but prioritize their happiness.*
- *Set a strong intention to slow down and savor life, rather than speed through it.*

Note that none of this is working on yourself!" (Lola Jones, page 170.)

"Savor the waiting. Enjoy the journey. That journey turns out to be your life."
Lola Jones

▶ PLAY ALONG: Don't Wait To Start Living

Waiting...

Waiting for enlightenment to start, waiting for your pain to depart, waiting for the rain to let up, waiting for your joy to wake up.

Waiting for the sun to come out, waiting for the tide to come in, waiting for your health to improve, waiting for this traffic to move.

Waiting for the week to end, waiting for your heart to mend, waiting for the day you are thin, waiting for your life to begin.

Life will be so much better then.

Now ask:

- "How fully can I occupy my waiting?"
- "What would happen if I showed up for it, completely?"
- "What if I replaced waiting with simply...living, and being?"
- "What if *Life* has been waiting on me to show up?"

Life marches to the beat of *Yes*. When you fall in step with it, magic truly begins.

Show the world how to be unconditionally happy.

Section Ten Mantra: Be Happy Now

GRACE IN ACTION

As your inner world continues to soften, lighten and expand, the outer world may not always understand or agree with you.

So many in our hardened, tough, sometimes-cruel world have forgotten their intrinsic power and worthiness. Caught up in fear and confusion, they let outer conditions determine their wellbeing. When their security is threatened (or perceived to be threatened), rather than going within to make things right, they make outer things wrong so they can feel right. Your increasing freedom, ease, and unconditional wellbeing may feel like a threat to some people's security, and they may try to make you wrong.

You have several choices:

You can break off your relationship with the world and avoid dealing with it.

You can push back and try to change the world by forcing it to understand the error of its ways (this is the worst use of your energy).

Or you can choose to accept the world just as it is and simply live your own most authentic, joyful life. This is by far the most challenging, powerful and liberating choice. You cannot make it but from the solid ground of true self-acceptance.

Increased self-acceptance happens naturally as your vibration moves up the emotional scale. Your own fears and confusion soften and begin to melt when you stop avoiding and resisting them. Eventually, inner security and sanity return, and you become increasingly invulnerable to the madness of this world. When you lower your defenses, the world's warring ways no longer challenge you the way they once did.

You cannot change the world if you remove yourself from it. And you only strengthen its ways if you play by its rules—by making it wrong to prove yourself right.

But if you become able to accept the world as it is, the world around you will begin to change. You become able when you becoming willing to love and accept yourself as you are—even as you are growing, changing and becoming more than you now are.

Don't let outer conditions determine your security and wellbeing. Claim your power. Decide to be as happy as you can right now, no matter what. *Show* the world how to be unconditionally happy. This is an exceptionally powerful form of activism.

Allow Grace to be trustworthy.
Be willing to let The Divine do the heavy lifting, and experience that it does.

Closing Invitation

How close can you get to this moment? Are you willing to discover what's really here? It's not what the mind thinks. Life isn't waiting to punish or wanting your penance; *No* is not part of Life's vocabulary. Life's arms are open wide, awaiting your surrender so it can meet your trust with trustworthiness. There is no other way life can respond but to meet you where you are.

How close can you get to this moment? No matter what is here, when you are willing to fall a little deeper into the experience you are having, you fall into Grace, over and over. Grace always catches you when you really let go. Sometimes your small self won't agree, but The Divine always has your back.

How close can you get to this moment? Say *Yes* to what is and find out. Say *Yes* and experience how life is kind, even when it's sometimes hard—and how your *Yes* assures a softer landing, wherever you might fall.

How close can you get to this moment? Let go, and find out. You don't have to know how. Just be willing to soften, again and again, and allow Grace to be trustworthy. Be willing to let The Divine do the heavy lifting, and experience that it does.

Endless Love,
Melinda

Quotation References

Many find it helpful to read a quotation in its native habitat. Below are the corresponding page numbers for each of the quotes listed on the blank journal pages throughout this *Playbook*. All *Things* page numbers are from the 2016 10th Anniversary edition of *Things Are Going Great In My Absence*.

Playbook Page	*Things* Page	*Playbook* Page	*Things* Page
10	12	94	90
12	10	98	77
14	26	100	73
16	26	104	89
18	51	108	91
22	20	110	92
24	24	114	99
28	28	116	108
32	35	120	104
34	42	124	120
36	35	126	106
38	38	128	111
40	32	130	105
42	31	132	104
46	40	134	106
48	42	138	111
54	46	140	116
56	49	142	116
58	51	144	118
60	39	146	121
62	39	150	124
64	52	154	131
68	46	160	137
72	42	162	140
74	79	166	147
82	53	168	152
84	115	170	154
86	74	172	171
88	77	174	152

Your Instrument Panel

Ecstasy
Joy, Bliss
Knowing, Empowerment
Freedom
Love, Appreciation
Passion, Eagerness, Enthusiasm, Happiness
Positive Expectation, Belief
Optimism, Can Do
Hopefulness, Seeing Possibility
Self Esteem, Courage

POWERFUL
In alignment with Large Self
Non-resistant
In the flow
EXPANDED
Relief
Relaxed
Softer
Allowing

Acceptance, Letting Go, Content, Relaxed
Boredom, Don't Care
Pessimism, Can't

No charge on it
- Resting Zone, Emptiness

Frustration, Irritation, Impatience - The Tipping Point

Overwhelm, Stressed

Disappointment
Doubt, Confusion, Uncertainty

Worry, Negative Thoughts
Blame, Project on Others

Discouragement, Quit, Fatigue

Anger - A Bridge To Regaining Your Power

Revenge   **FIGHT**
Hatred/Rage
Jealousy, Desire that doesn't feel good, Craving
Fear
                                           FLIGHT
Grief, Sadness, Regret, Shame
Unworthiness, despair, apathy, numbness   FROZEN

RELIEF is always that way! ↑

All emotions are
Divine Energy at
different frequencies.

Mantra: All feelings
are good.

Resistant
Tense
Harder
Against the flow
CONTRACTED

Out of alignment with
Large Self

Influenced by the teachings of Abraham/Jerry and Esther Hicks, and David R. Hawkins, Power vs. Force

Divine Openings.com   Lola Jones

Melinda Gates spent decades trying to fix herself until she discovered *Things Are Going Great In My Absence* in 2009 and stepped into a new story: she was not broken! She learned new ways of thinking and feeling that made sense, and her life changed in remarkable ways. In two years, addictions fell away, depression lifted, and significant health and financial crises turned around.

Since then, Melinda has experienced how the words in *Things Are Going Great In My Absence*—and the experiences they point to—endlessly deepen and expand. And she knows, beyond doubt, that showing up, being as light and playful as she can, and letting Grace do the heavy lifting are the only invitations Life needs to reveal its magic.

Melinda's desire to write this *Playbook* most definitely did not arise from lack: *Things Are Going Great In My Absence* doesn't need clarification or help in saying what it says and doing what it does. Instead, this book emerged from the fulfillment of its possibilities and promises—and Melinda's heartfelt desire to share and invite others to experience the freedom and unconditional wellbeing that Divine Openings has made possible for her.

As founder and steward of Divine Openings, I'm delighted to introduce Melinda Gates and recommend her Divine Openings Playbook. For all of you who have or are about to read my foundational Divine Openings book, Things Are Going Great In My Absence, or if you're in the Level 1 Online Course, let Melinda's Playbook help you develop your own wisdom through self-expression, contemplation, and experiential activities—applying the book to whatever is going on in your life right now. Melinda powerfully shares her own experience, her stumbles as well as her successes, and shows you how to use whatever happens in your daily life to take you higher. You'll especially love it if you've "done it all" and are looking for a new way to play and go deeper while reviewing the basics.—Lola Jones, author of Things Are Going Great In My Absence and creator of Divine Openings

Melinda has a gift for creating space for others to transform in—I know she does this brilliantly in her one-on-one sessions, and she's done the same thing here with this Playbook. This is a wonderful companion to Lola Jones's Things Are Going Great In My Absence, and it truly reflects what Melinda does best: creating space for you to go deeper.— Donna Wetterstrand, Divine Openings Guide and Head of the Certified Guide Program

In Things Are Going Great In My Absence, by Lola Jones, readers awaken to Divine Grace and get to know the address of pure joy, by heart. In Melinda Gates's radiant companion guide, The Divine Openings Playbook, readers enjoy clear guidance that further deepens our relationship with Lola Jones's teachings, with ourselves, and with Divine Grace. It invites us to "play along!" Melinda's genuine compassion flows through the Playbook—especially her sensitivity to the games the mind sometimes plays. She shines a light on major points in Things Are Going Great In My Absence, and encourages us to journal, play, grow, dance, and to really…finally…let go. A true companion.—Jill Cooper, author of The Yes Book

How delicious! Thank you Melinda for giving us such a joyful possibility to stay even more tuned in to the Divine Openings process. I love your book. I am touched by your honesty and clarity. It reminds me just at the right moment to say yes to everything and to feel the feelings showing up. It is so powerful and brings us even deeper into our Large Self perspective.—Angelika Lukoschek, Divine Openings Guide and German Certified Guide Program Mentor

What a gift to all of us. As a Divine Openings Guide holding regular book-groups and guiding a lot of my clients into a deeper understanding of Divine Openings, this book offers all the information and practical steps needed. It feels like you've put into writing what I try to convey to my Divine Openings family step by step over the past year. With this book, I hold in my hands a summary of everything my small self wishes to be able to let go of, so the Divine can do the heavy lifting. What a comfort and joy! This book sends out rays of light into the world. Please receive my gratitude for bringing it into manifestation!—Anita Kriz, Divine Openings Guide, Austria

This book is a perfect companion to Lola's book. It offers various options to go even deeper and touches both your brain and your soul. Helpful repetitions bring you closer and closer to the core messages of Lola's book and finally to the Divine within yourself. Melinda, I love your style of writing; it's both inspiring and entertaining.—Ulrich Kriz, Divine Openings Guide, Austria

Melinda Gates's delightful <u>Playbook</u> represents and illustrates beautifully how to embrace the Divine Openings experience more in our daily lives. A treasure trove of activities, thoughts, and embodied action, this book truly gives the reader a way to live more richly in this precious life that we live. I highly recommend it for both new and advanced people in Divine Openings and know that wherever you are on your path, it will deepen your experience, as it did mine.—Verity, singer/songwriter

Thank you so much for this generous gift. I'm really touched that you've shared your wonderful, insightful, beautifully written work with me. There is so much wisdom, clarity and much-needed guidance, and I feel your beautiful energy lifting the words off the page in a joyful dance of universal truth. It feels like gentle, nourishing rain on my parched soul. How lucky I am to have this, and you, as a companion as I navigate life.—Gina Hetherington, writer